PRAISE FOR

The Wine Seeker's Guide to Livermore Valley

While on assignment with Tom on a beautiful trip to Tahiti and Bora Bora I got to know him as a passionate travel writer and photographer. But as an Italian and lover of good wines I am now in awe of the depth of history and culture which accompanies the reader well beyond the taste of Bacchus' nectar in *The Wine Seeker's Guide to Livermore Valley*.

—SILVIA BIZIO, LA REPUBBLICA DAILY NEWSPAPER, ITALY

Tom Wilmer brings his award-winning style to a surprisingly un-known area for wine tour adventures...The next time I find my-self in San Francisco, I'll be slipping out of town with *The Wine Seeker's Guide to Livermore Valley* and then some serious sipping can start.

—MAX WOOLDRIDGE, ACTIVE & ADRENALIN WRITER—THE MAIL ON SUNDAY, LONDON

Here we sit on the East Coast, sippin' on a five buck Noveau Red while skimming through our old buddy Tom Wilmer's new *Wine Seeker's Guide to Livermore Valley*. He once again has us dreaming of sliding into a ragtop rental with a lovely companion to experience first-hand his latest worthy guide.

—BOB KAPPSTATTER, NY DAILY NEWS

Margaret and I had the pleasure of spending time with Tom when he visited our beautiful Barossa wine region in South Australia. His sub-sequent Barossa story showed his real strengths: the ability to connect with our community and to truly tell our stories. He has brought this very same gift to *The Wine Seeker's Guide to Livermore Valley* and when we read it, we felt we had been given a very special invitation to discover Livermore Valley.

—PETER LEHMANN, PETER LEHMANN WINES, BAROSSA VALLEY, SOUTH AUSTRALIA

Mon Dieu! Does the world need another wine book? Believe it or not, it needs this one. Thomas C. Wilmer's *The Wine Seeker's Guide to Livermore Valley*...reminds me of an afternoon's long, comfort-filled conversation with a savvy but generous friend eager to share with new-old friends his enthusiasm for good things: culture, cuisine, community, art, history; all those qualities that pair so well with fine wines and *la dolce vita*....Yes; the world, especially the California corner of it, needed this book.

—Georgia I. Hesse, founding editor of the *SF Examiner Travel Section*, contributing writer, *San Francisco Chronicle*, *Nob Hill Gazette*

In this comprehensive presentation of one of California's most historic fine wine regions, Tom Wilmer has provided Wine Seeker's with an invaluable resource that will lead them to the special wineries and the profoundly enjoyable lifestyle of the Livermore Valley. This work is a must for locals and visitors alike who wish to explore and enjoy one of California's most edifying terroirs.

—Archie McLaren, Founder & Chairman, Central Coast Wine Classic

The Wine Seeker's Guide to Livermore Valley inspires me to explore this area and the wonderful wineries! I found it easy to read, very detailed and I know it will be a tremendous new resource. This area is clearly a hidden jewel!

—Jon Kimball, General Manager & Area Managing Director, The Westin St. Francis, San Francisco

The Livermore Valley is a diverse, historical, and under-appreciated appellation. Tom did a great job weaving the various winery stories into a compelling narrative about the 150 years of wine crafting history that makes the Livermore Valley so special. With a writing style that is, at once, engaging and factual and a layout that is beautiful and accessible, Tom has created a book that I'm sure will be very valuable to the Livermore wineries and very interesting for their guests. Tom Wilmer loves wine and is passionate about writing. I can't think of a more fitting combination to help bring alive the stories of our area's wine history.

—Steven Mirassou Owner, Steven Kent Winery, La Rochelle Winery

Tom Wilmer's *Wine Seeker's Guide to Livermore Valley* is a complete and practical guide to our wine country that will be of great benefit to both first-time tourists and locals who have not visited all the wonderful wine adventures available in this Valley. It is a frank and straightforward approach that provides a wealth of information on taking advantage of the best the region has to offer, an indispensible guide that every wine region must have.

—Phil Wente, Wente Vineyards

The perfect follow-up to Tom Wilmer's *Romancing the Coast* guide to California inns, resorts and B&Bs, is his *The Wine Seeker's Guide to Livermore Valley*. Tom does his research and shares his knowledge with style and charm.

—KIM COOL, AUTHOR OF THE *COOL ROAD TRIP* SERIES OF
FLORIDA GUIDEBOOKS AND *VENICE HISTORY ILLUSTRATED*

Tom has used his expertise to distill onto the page the many aspects that make our appellation and individual wineries the valuable and interesting wine seeker's destination that we are today. The Livermore Valley, with its long history of fine wines and dedication to the industry, is beautifully represented in this book. It should grace all wine lovers' coffee tables and a second copy should be in the glove box of the car in which you go wine tasting on the weekends.

—DANE STARK, PAGE MILL WINERY, LIVERMORE CALIFORNIA

As I read the proofs for *Wine Seeker's Guide to Livermore Valley* I was very impressed with the writing style of the author, Tom Wilmer. He writes in an honest refined fashion, unlike so many "in your face" articles written in wine magazines.

—EMILIE COYNE, PRESIDENT, THOMAS COYNE WINERY, LIVERMORE CALIFORNIA

Tom Wilmer's *Wine Seeker's Guide to Livermore Valley* is a great resource for locals and tourists coming to visit the growing and historic Livermore Valley. Tom captures each winery's unique story in an honest, entertaining fashion. He leaves you with enough information, but intrigues you to go visit the winery in person. Each narrative is candid and captures the wineries story perfectly.

—HEATHER MCGRAIL LORIER, MCGRAIL VINEYARDS
AND WINERY, LIVERMORE, CALIFORNIA

The Wine Seeker's Guide to Livermore Valley opens the door to a refreshing new wine tasting experience. This is wine country, close to all San Francisco cities, yet surprisingly rural. The author is thorough in his presentation of wineries, winemakers and wine, yet writes in a readable style. The guide is a must in preparing for a relaxing and exciting weekend of tasting in the Livermore Valley.

—NANCY MOLYNEAUX, OWNER RODRIGUE MOLYNEAUX WINERY, LIVERMORE CALIFORNIA

Wine Seeker's Guide to Livermore Valley chronicles the region's rich winemaking history, presents information about all the local wineries and highlights the many recreational and cultural opportunities in the area. A special section dedicated to The Rose Hotel showcases our historical roots, our world-class design and amenities and our connection to the Madden family.

—COACH JOHN MADDEN'S ROSE HOTEL IN PLEASANTON

I've had the pleasure of sipping a glass (or two) with Tom Wilmer in the Livermore Valley, as well as other wine country tasting rooms. Tom is a warm and engaging guy, and that feeling comes through in his comprehensive coverage of this historic wine region. Cheers.

—GLEN PUTMAN, TRAVEL EDITOR, *GENTRY* MAGAZINE

Tom Wilmer gives you a real taste of Livermore Valley from the pages of his guide. He is adeptly able to paint a picture of each winery, making this a great resource when you visit the region. You immediately get a feel for each producer from the witty taglines and enticing photography. This book is a must while you are planning a visit.

—REBECCA CHAPA, WINE EDUCATOR AND CONSULTANT, TANNIN MANAGEMENT

A complete visitor's guide and more: Wilmer's book tells the collective personal story of winemaking in this historic, burgeoning, undersung California wine region. Through individual snapshots, he describes the winemaking path, approach to the craft, and personality of each place. *The Wine Seeker's Guide* will put you on the fast track to being a Livermore Valley wine insider.

—SARA SCHNEIDER, WINE EDITOR, *SUNSET MAGAZINE*

The Wine Seeker's Guide to

Livermore Valley

LIVERMORE VALLEY
Wine Country

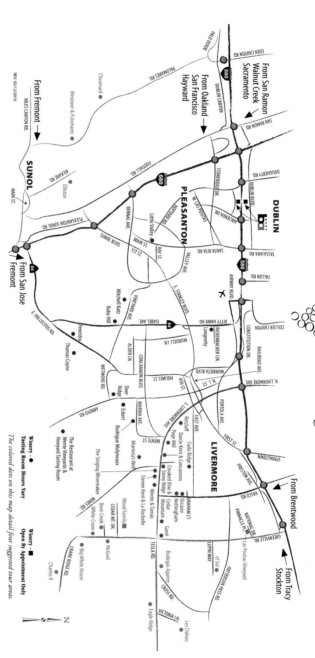

Livermore Valley Wine Country is located along Interstates 580 and 680 just east of San Francisco. Our wine country includes wineries in Livermore, Pleasanton, Sunol and Castro Valley. It is easily accessible by air via the San Francisco, San Jose and Oakland airports. BART (Bay Area Rapid Transit) also serves the Tri-Valley.

An **American Viticultural Area (AVA)** is an official federally designated grape growing region. Each AVA encompasses unique growing climates and soil composition. There are over 170 AVA's in the United States. The Livermore Valley AVA includes the cities of Danville, Dublin, Livermore, Pleasanton, San Ramon, and the eastern boundaries of Castro Valley and Sunol.

REV. 02/12/2010

The colored dots on this map detail four suggested tour areas.

Winery -
Tasting Room Hours Vary

Winery -
Open By Appointment Only

The Wine Seeker's Guide to
Livermore Valley

Thomas C. Wilmer

RiverWood Books
Ashland, Oregon

RiverWood Books
PO Box 3400
Ashland, OR 97520
www.riverwoodbooks.com

First printing: 2010

Cover and interior design by Confluence Book Services
Cover images by Steven F. Kelly (background), Wente Vineyards (golfer), John Montgomery (barrel image), and Tyler Vu Photography (wedding image)

Printed in Korea

Library of Congress Cataloging-in-Publication Data

Wilmer, Thomas C., 1949-
  The wine seeker's guide to Livermore Valley / by Thomas C. Wilmer.
-- 1st ed.
        p. cm.
  Includes bibliographical references and index.
  ISBN-13: 978-0-9793840-2-8 (pbk. : alk. paper)
  ISBN-10: 1-883991-69-2 (alk. paper)
  1. Wine and wine making--California--Livermore Valley--Guide-books. 2. Wineries--California--Livermore Valley--Guidebooks. 3. Livermore Valley (Calif.)--Guidebooks. I. Title.
  TP557.W686 2010
  641.2'20979465--dc22
                                        2010015404

Contents

Acknowledgements

To my wife, Beth, who remained supportive and encouraging throughout the entire field research and writing process, which often entailed weeklong stays in Livermore Valley.

To my editor at RiverWood Books, Raina Hassan, one of those rare word surgeons who will insert the absolutely perfect word that replaces three of yours. Raina's most impressive quality is her ability to tweak and tune and manicure while leaving the author's voice and style totally intact—only way better than at the outset. To Christy Collins, the creative director at RiverWood Books, who was responsible for bringing the diverse content and design elements together. From her elegant cover, to the drop-dead beautiful interior layout, eye-catching photographic placement, and awesome font-utilization, Ms. Collins singlehandedly created a most impressive visual work of art.

This book would still be a work in progress if it were not for the priceless support and assistance provided by the Livermore Valley Wine Growers Association—most notably, Executive Director Chris Chandler and her staff—Andrea Branton, Kathy Liske, Traci Anderson, and Brandi Addington, who handled all of my weekly interview schedules, complete with detailed Excel spreadsheets. They also arranged meetings with personalities who normally shield themselves from the public, and they spent untold hours in search of stock and archival historic photography. They also cheerfully arranged overnight accommodations at Livermore's Hawthorn Suites when needed. Whatever my request, from arranging a meeting with Livermore City Historian Garret Drummond to a meeting with Carolyn and Phil Wente, all I had to do was ask and it was done. Ms. Chandler's daunting task of arranging more than fifty interviews leading into harvest and throughout crush earned her the amply deserved title "Cat Herder Extraordinaire." I owe her and the association a profound thank you!

Priceless thanks to the *Independent Magazine* for offering extensive use of their superb stock images, and the Livermore Heritage Guild for providing the historic photography. We are also indebted to local and regional professional photographers, including John Montgomery, Barbara Mallon, Annie Tao, and Steven F. Kelly who graciously supplied their excellent images.

Ms. Phylis Grisham, General Manager, and Tom Walker, Director of Sales, at the John Madden family's Rose Hotel in downtown Pleasanton: gracious thanks for extending overnight accommodations anytime I asked. When I mentioned to Ms. Grisham that I'd like to meet with John Madden's son, Mike, there he was—waiting for me in the lobby the following morning. They also provided savvy insider recommendations and directions to discover the best things to see and do in downtown Pleasanton and throughout the region.

To every one of the Livermore Valley winery owners, winemakers, and growers—a really big, bold, fruit forward thank you! Everybody was so helpful and supportive and enthused about the book project, and they went out of their way to help me understand the nuances of grape growing and winemaking in Livermore Valley. It was refreshing and touching to discover that the Livermore Valley wine industry intimately understands that everyone wins by promoting one another.

Livermore winery owner and ardent hiker Nancy Rodrigue has spent the past thirty years traversing virtually every trail and nook and cranny in the valley, and she graciously agreed to write the regional hiking section. She is also co-author of a new Livermore Valley hiking guidebook, *Tri-Valley Trails*, along with co-author Jacky Poulsen. Thank you, Nancy!

Kudos to Cal Poly Soil Science Professor Tom Rice for penning the brilliant Livermore Valley Terroir piece and offering excerpts from his new book, *Paso Robles: An American Terroir*.

A debt of gratitude is owed to Ms. Sandy Sims, fellow Bay Area Travel Writers board member. Sandy cheerfully researched and wrote the bulk of the Things to Do and See section. Her invaluable contributions, including numerous forays to visit and inspect a litany of businesses, allowed me to maintain my primary focus on researching and writing the winery and winemaker profiles.

Thanks to my Intern/Research Assistant Brittnee Miles Clark for all of her wonderful contributions.

Most touching of all is that in concluding the writing process, I've realized that I now have a barrel full of wonderful new friends throughout the Livermore Valley wine world, and I cherish that thought.

Wente Foreword

*T*he Livermore Valley holds a unique distinction among the many prestigious valleys of the California Coastal Range—an area that immediately attracted many of the early wine industry's innovators. Beginning a mere five miles from the San Francisco Bay, it is one of only two California coastal valleys that run from east to west. It's situated between 4,000-foot mountains to the south and north, and it is this unique geography that channels the cool westerly marine breezes from the Pacific Ocean into the Livermore Valley. Powered by the icy waters of the Pacific, these wind-streams rush through the Golden Gate and sweep across the bay, delivering a blanket of fog that literally rolls over the Oakland-Hayward ridgeline and nestles onto the Livermore Valley floor. The fog usually lingers for several hours each morning before yielding to the warm afternoons and later cooling the valley just before sunset. The natural phenomena of this area inspired visionary pioneers to confidently plant classic grape varieties—and they quickly earned the first three major international awards for California wine in

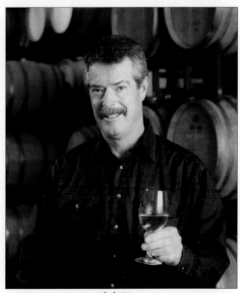

Phil Wente

the World Expositions of 1889, 1915, and 1937, long before the Paris tasting of 1976. Great vineyards are the key to excellent wines, and the combination of the range of marine-influenced climates and well-drained soils have allowed a tradition of unparalleled vineyards to thrive.

Today, the Livermore Valley is internationally known for a wide variety of significant accomplishments and natural resources. Foremost among them is the quality of life enhanced by beautiful vineyards, outstanding wines, and five unique towns that offer endless opportunities to explore and enjoy all the best that wine country has to offer. From operations with more than 125 years of winegrowing history to the passion and energy of newly founded ventures, more than fifty wineries proudly put out their welcome signs and offer visitors outstanding hospitality. Beautiful state and regional parks, bicycle trails, equestrian activities, performing arts theaters, festivals, rodeos, and friendly people await you here. Come explore the history, culture, cuisine, and passion of the Livermore Valley. I invite you to visit, taste, dine, and stay.

—Phil Wente, Fourth-Generation Winegrower

Concannon Foreword

The Livermore Valley wine community has achieved a well-deserved reputation for producing world-class wine. It has earned recognition for its years of social responsibility and great commitment to programs and stewardship of the land. This acclaim emerged from the rich heritage of each family's dedication to values and high technical standards.

It is historically documented that wine grapes have been grown in the Livermore Valley since the 1840s, but the vineyard explosion that started in 1882 catapulted Livermore Valley to the front ranks of American wine regions.

In 1883 a favorable land report by Charles Wetmore to the state Viticulture Commission compared the natural conditions of the Livermore Valley to some of the great wine regions of France.

By the mid-1890s Livermore had well over a hundred vineyards and more than 4,000 acres under vine, a level not reached again until a full century later.

My grandfather James Concannon purchased his first forty-seven acres in 1882. He built the family home that four generations of family grew up in. The home has been renovated and still stands today.

James Concannon

He planted his vineyard a year later, thus establishing Concannon Vineyard, which has been continuously producing wine under the same family label since 1883.

Urban expansion has put some California wine regions like Livermore Valley at risk. To combat this expansion and with an eye on protecting our viticultural heritage, Concannon and other Livermore Valley vineyard holders have put their land in a legal trust that strictly prohibits any future urban development.

Our new Concannon Conservancy wines are sourced from these vineyards now protected forever from urban encroachment.

Thus, our shared desire to preserve the Livermore Valley's winemaking heritage will assure the production of rich and flavorful wines for generations to come!

—James Concannon, Third-Generation Vintner

Introduction

In many respects, Livermore Valley is the unsung historical incubator of California's wine industry. Valley vintners have been quietly producing world-class wines for more than 125 years, and they've contributed many industry-wide innovations and firsts in both wine growing and production.

There are many savvy wine seekers who religiously trek to the valley for weekend getaways, day-trip tasting adventures, and the numerous annual festivals and concerts. Leisurely wending through the Livermore Valley Wine Trail—sans traffic jams and crowds—is rejuvenating and unforgettable.

*I*f you visit wineries here, odds are excellent that you will have the pleasure to meet and visit with the winery owners and winemakers. *The Wine Seeker's Guide to Livermore Valley* is the first book to showcase this enchanting region's winemakers, growers, and winery owners. This book is not simply about their varieties, growing practices, and *terroirs*—although you'll read about that, too. These pages also contain the stories and passions of the people who are the lifeblood of the Livermore Valley wine industry.

We've also included an enticing *Things to Do and See* section, which includes suggestions for shopping, hiking, eating, and more, including places to stay and local events. While exploring the region, you can ride on the historic Niles Canyon Wine Train, enjoy a memorable dinner at Wente Vineyards' award-winning restaurant, visit museums and galleries, and settle in for a cozy stay at the sumptuous Rose Hotel in downtown Pleasanton. Between visits to the area's wineries, you might enjoy an evening concert, take a leisurely stroll through one of the many seasonal festivals, and explore the enchanting towns of Livermore, Pleasanton, Dublin, San Ramon, Danville, Sunol, Castro Valley and the many other alluring destinations throughout the Livermore Valley American Viticulture Area (AVA).

While doing my own exploring here, I realized something: The Livermore Valley wine experience is not just about wine. It's really more about partnership and family—husbands and wives, fathers and sons, grandparents and grandchildren, all working side by side. And they're not simply growing grapes and producing wine. Through this work, they create and strengthen the bonds of culture and family, and, ultimately, a sense of community.

It might be surprising to you, but many of these families are not in the business only to produce high-quality wines. Many of them savor the fun and friendships, both old and new. For them, it's about enjoying fine food, listening to musicians perform everything from reggae to rock n' roll, and sharing a passion for the arts—from sculpture to oils to photography. Wine functions as the thematic thread—the catalyst, the tie that binds the community together. Ask most Livermore Valley winery owners why they're in the profession, and the word "fun" will likely show up in their reply.

Like most people with a passion for the wine world (whether growers, producers, or consumers), those in the Livermore Valley wine community have an Old-World style of living and socializing. They navigate through a universe where wine rarely stands alone. It is an integral part of their daily lives. The ideal is to serve and savor wine with hors d'oeuvres and multi-course meals under the stars, accompanied by live music. The experience can last for hours.

One of the blessings of Livermore Valley's wine growers is their unexploited innocence. They craft wines that stand up to the best of Napa, Sonoma, and other renowned California growing regions, but their AVA (America's seventeenth appellation to receive formal American Viticultural Area designation back in 1982) remains largely unheralded.

Fifteen miles long by ten miles wide, the AVA is defined by deep, well drained gravelly soils and maritime influences. Many people, only vaguely familiar with the region, assume that the climate is similar to California's interior San Joaquin Valley, with its roasting-hot summer days and sultry nights. Livermore Valley is a coastal environment and an integral part of the legendary Central Coast AVA winegrowing appellation (stretching south to Santa Barbara County), as well as the San Francisco Bay AVA. The rare east-west orientation of the valley's coastal mountains allows marine air and fog to flow through the Golden Gate and into the valley during the evening, creating warm days and cool nights—optimum conditions for producing the valley's award-winning Bordeaux, Rhone, Spanish, Portuguese, and Tuscan-style wines.

The valley is also blessed with a breadth of microclimates. On the westside, temperatures average as much as 10 to 15 degrees cooler than the eastside, where vines tend to produce more intense, fruitier grapes in contrast to the western fringe's leaner, softer fruit expression.

Signature Livermore Valley varieties include Petite Sirah, Syrah, Zinfandel, Sangiovese, Tempranillo, Barbera, Pinot Grigio, Pinot Noir, Merlot, Cabernet Sauvignon, Cabernet Blanc, Cabernet Franc, Sauvignon Blanc, and Chardonnay.

Welcome to the timeless, off-the-beaten-path Livermore Valley wine country. I hope you'll enjoy reading about the wineries featured here—the owners, winemakers, and their superb wines.

Cheers to seeking and discovering all that you hope to find in this enchanting part of our world.

—Thomas C. Wilmer

Notes from Livermore Valley's Wine History

One of the most auspicious occasions in California's viticultural history happened in 1889—not in California, but at the grand Paris Exposition (celebrating the one hundredth anniversary of the French Revolution). The story of how this moment came to pass stretches back to Livermore Valley in the 1830s.

According to the Livermore City Historian, Garrett Drummond, local wine production in the mid-1800s was crude at best. "It was a case of quantity over quality."

Livermore's Bustelli-Canton manufacturer of redwood wine barrels

Livermore Valley's first vintner, Jose Maria Amador (namesake of Amador County), planted 1,500 vines on his rancho in 1832. Robert Livermore was reported to have grape arbors fronting his ranch house in 1840. Amador; Livermore; Alfonso Ladd, who maintained a small vineyard on his property as early as 1864; and John Kottinger with his circa-1874, four-acre Pleasanton vineyard, all grew Mission varietal grapes.*

The advent of the Transcontinental Railroad in 1869, with station stops in Livermore Valley, dramatically increased the market reach of all local agrarian enterprises. Although as recently as 1880, Drummond says, less than fifty acres in the entire valley were devoted to grapes. But all that would soon change, and rapidly, with the arrival of UC Berkeley graduate Charles Wetmore.

As a correspondent for the Alta, California, newspaper in 1878, Wetmore conducted a study of the state's wine industry and found it depressed and in dire need of education—in both growing practices and winemaking expertise.

Wetmore journeyed to France and spent more than a year studying European viticultural methodology. He returned home armed with a sophisticated understanding of ideal soil conditions, optimum varieties suited to specific terroir, vine cultivation, and proper field practices to guarantee the best grapes possible.

One of Wetmore's most brilliant moves was to return home with cuttings from the legendary Château d'Yquem, located in Bordeaux's Sauternes district. The revered sweet Château d'Yquem Sauternes wine is a late-harvest Semillon that is positively influenced by a helpful mold, *Botrytis Cinerea* (fondly referred to as Noble Rot).

Wetmore's term as secretary of the California Viticultural Commission, combined with his freshly acquired knowledge of the Old Country's wine industry, equipped him with an astute awareness of the regions with optimum viticultural potential. He selected Livermore Valley to plant his Semillon and opened the Cresta Blanca

Winery in 1882. According to Drummond, Wetmore selected Livermore because he realized that the soil and environmental conditions were remarkably similar to the premier vineyards of France, especially those in the Bordeaux region.

Around the same time, a perfect confluence of social, political, economic, and religious upheavals throughout Western Europe drove some of the best and brightest to seek their fortunes in the New World. Among the newcomers who sailed across the Atlantic and worked their way out West were Carl Heinrich Wente from Northern Germany and James Concannon, a native of Ireland's Aran Islands. Both found prophetic opportunities awaiting them in the San Francisco Bay Area.

Wente went to work for Charles Krug in Napa Valley, where he learned the craft of growing and processing grapes, while Concannon, living in San Francisco's Mission

Armstrong pump

Adrian Chauche's Mont-Rouge winery and vineyards, established in 1884, won a gold medal at the 1889 Paris Exposition.

Bottling and labeling at Charles Wetmore's Cresta Blanca Winery. Founded in 1882, it won the 1889 Paris Exposition Grand Prix award.

District, developed a close friendship with the city's first Catholic Archbishop, Joseph Alemany.

Following Alemany's suggestion, Concannon planted grapes and opened a winery to supply the Catholic Church with sacramental wine. In 1883, Wente and Concannon both commenced their Livermore Valley vineyard operations—and both grew to become two of the most legendary names in California's wine industry.

The Paris Exposition

The year was 1889, and Livermore vintners stormed the world stage when they entered their wines—along with 17,000 other contenders from around the globe—at the International Paris Exposition wine contest.

Wetmore blew away the competition when his Livermore Valley Cresta Blanca Sauternes claimed the coveted Grande Prix and a gold medal. Adrian Chauche's Livermore Valley Mont-Rouge was also awarded a gold medal, and a Napa vintner walked away with a third gold.

By 1890 the race was on. Livermore Valley's reputation was stellar, and the area was exploding with new growers and wineries.

Olivina's ivy-clad cellars

Photo courtesy of *The Livermore Heritage Guild*

A Glimpse of the Great Olivina Farm

By 1893, Drummond says, "The State Viticultural Commission reported 121 vineyards, encompassing 4,466 acres in Livermore Valley, along with 23 onsite wine producers, with a combined cooperage capacity of 1.4 million gallons."

Drummond notes that only six Livermore winemakers—Olivina, Ruby Hill, Château Bellevue, Concannon, Wente Brothers, and Cresta Blanca—bottled and labeled their own product. The majority sold their grapes to local vintners or shipped their product in bulk railcars, while Wente bottled at their winery facility in Richmond, California.

The trend-setting achievements of Livermore Valley continued throughout the twentieth century and into the present. The Wente family brought the first Chardonnay clones from France in 1912 and introduced that wine to America. Wente also offered the first varietally labeled Sauvignon Blanc in 1935. Today, more than 80 percent of the Chardonnay plantings across California are Wente clones. And Concannon was the first in America to produce varietally labeled Petite Sirah.

Concannon Vineyards (Patriarch James Concannon in white apron)

Prohibition decimated the wine industry, and only those who produced sacramental and medicinal wines, such as Concannon and Wente, as well as a handful who marketed table grapes, survived.

After Prohibition, Livermore Valley producers immediately set out to re-establish the wine industry. It took some time, as Drummond points out. "Prohibition caused a substantial decrease in wine consumption across America. Few retailers were selling wine, and few restaurant waiters were familiar with quality wines—hard liquor had taken the lead." When Roosevelt repealed the Eighteenth Amendment in 1933 there were fewer than 1,200 acres under cultivation in the valley, and it was less than ten years ago that the acreage and number of wineries in Livermore Valley began to approach the pre-Prohibition heyday.

From the mid-1930s on, Wente and Concannon aggressively planted and promoted one of the largest assemblages of premium varieties in California. Concannon showcased Sauvignon Blanc, Petite Sirah, and Semillon, while Wente promoted Sauvignon Blanc, Grey Riesling, Pinot Chardonnay, and Semillon. In technical endeavors, Wente experimented with overhead irrigation and was the first to introduce mechanical harvesters.

Today's enthusiasm, energy, ever-increasing momentum, and most notably the incredible grapes and wines produced by the area's vintners, has set the stage for another exciting chapter in Livermore Valley's wine history.

Ferrario

Ruby Hill

Photos courtesy of The Livermore Heritage Guild

* The Spanish Mission grape (vinifera Monica or Criolla) was first introduced to California in 1769 by Padre Serra at Mission San Diego. The Mission varietal was legendary as a mediocre wine (although it still exists, and savvy winemakers tell me it can make some of the most awesome Angelica on the planet).

A Working Definition of Terroir

M any words have multiple definitions. If you examine a dictionary, you will find that some words have seven or more meanings. Each definition has its unique place when using a specific word in conversation, in writing, or in just thinking about it. The word *terroir* (pronounced "tair-wah"), is no exception. Indeed, you will rarely find it in English dictionaries since it is a French term.

For every word, it is helpful to understand its evolution in order to better utilize it appropriately. The early roots of terroir originate from the Latin word, terra, literally meaning earth or land. Many other words also have this same root; e.g., terrace, terrain, terrarium, terrestrial, territory, terror and terrorist. It's curious that a word first used to define earth's land surface has evolved to define persons who defend land from invasion and even strive to acquire new lands by force. Such are the natures of our human languages.

Therefore, it is not surprising to find that terroir has many different definitions depending upon the context in which it is used. Many learned scholars have written about terroir and its multiple definitions. Today, viticulturists, enologists and marketers use the term to define the entire environment of their grape growing regions and to apply it to the unique regional flavors of their wines. Terroir ultimately is used by most persons to express a "sense of place." The Terroir-France web site asserts that "a terroir is a group of vineyards (or even vines) from the same region, belonging to a specific appellation, and sharing the same type of soil, weather conditions, grapes and winemaking savoir-faire, which contribute to give its specific personality to the wine." Moran (2006) has provided us a comprehensive examination of the many facets of terroir. He considers the human influence on terroir from the cultivation of land, to selection of plant materials, to the many choices made by the winemaker, from barrel selection to the aging time of the wine, and even to the marketing of wine. If these many facets of terroir are to be evaluated and quantified in a scientific context, the variables become too numerous. Therefore, the only unbiased, reasonable methods for terroir comparisons among vineyards or wine regions are "blind" wine tastings.

In this book (and at the risk of trying to define an undefinable concept), our working definition for terroir is "the measurable ecosystem variables of a vineyard or a geographic region, where a community of organisms (wine grapevines, their human managers and related biota) interacts with the earth's natural environment in the production of wine grapes."

—Thomas J. Rice, PhD, C.P.S.S.
Professor of Soil Science
Certified Professional Soil Scientist No. 1932
California Polytechnic State University

(Excerpted from *Paso Robles: An American Terroir* by Thomas J. Rice)

Darcie Kent

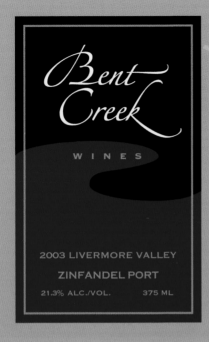

Bent Creek Winery
5455 Greenville Road
Livermore, CA 94550
(925) 455-6320

Website:
www.bentcreekwinery.com
Email: bentcreekwinery @
bentcreekwinery.com
Facebook

- Tasting room: Friday–Sunday, noon–4:30

- Visits: Monday–Thursday by appointment
  (925) 989-9610

- Established: 2002

- Owners: Tom and Pat Heineman, Rich (winemaker) and
  Carol Howell

- Annual production: 3,500 cases

- Varieties: Sauvignon Blanc, Chardonnay, Cabernet
  Franc, Cabernet Sauvignon, Zinfandel, Syrah (Bent
  Creek Vineyard), Petite Sirah, Syrah/Cabernet Sauvignon
  blend, vintage Port, Zinfandel Port (Bent Creek
  Vineyard), Petite Sirah Port (Bent Creek Vineyard)

- Wine club: First Call Wine Club

Good times start at the end of the road

*I*t all began with great vines. In 1996, Tom Heineman planted twelve acres of Syrah and then secured a rare, five-year-purchase contract with Concannon Vineyards. Subsequently, Tom and his wife, Pat, realizing the extraordinary quality of their fruits, decided to process and sell their own wine.

Today, award-winning Bent Creek produces estate-grown Syrah, Petite Sirah, and Zinfandel. The locally sourced Cabernet and Chardonnay may as well be estate grown—85 percent of Bent Creek's purchased grapes come from fields adjoining their fence line.

The vision behind Bent Creek's 2002 inception was a blend of the partners' personal passions. Three of the four were Livermore School District teachers and principals, while Rich Howell was a physicist at Livermore Labs. A shared love of wine led to the perfect melding of responsibilities for the two couples' second careers.

Iowa native Tom Heineman is a deft steward of the land who tenaciously believes that great wine is first made on the vine. He

Fall at Bent Creek Winery

goes to great lengths to ensure sustainable field practices, including drip irrigation and no-till soil conservation, and uses organic products to mitigate mold. "We respect the land," Tom says, summing up his philosophy.

Pat Heineman and Carol Howell are two vivacious and detail-oriented managers of the tasting room and wine club, and Rich Howell commenced his viticultural endeavors back in grad school when he started making wine in carboys during the wee hours between studies.

Once the four partners made a commitment to open the winery and tasting room, they began a series of intensive studies at UC Davis and UC Santa Cruz, which included coursework in enology, viticultural practices, winemaking, wine chemistry, and tasting room practices.

Winemaker Rich Howell details Bent Creek's winemaking vision, "Since day one we've remained dedicated to crafting small lots of complex wine primarily from

Award-winning wines at Bent Creek

Aerial view at Bent Creek Winery

Outside the winery tasting room

the grapes grown in our own vineyard and nearby Livermore Valley vineyards."

Rich says that they make wine the old-fashioned way beginning with open topped fermentation in half-ton bins. "We 'punch it down' by hand twice a day, and treat the wine gently during its two-year oak barrel aging process. Once the wine has been blended and bottled, we prefer to age it in the bottles for another year before release."

A visit to Bent Creek reveals the true essence of the partners' passion for the wine world and where their real payback resides: their love of interacting with people, fine food, and having fun is evident. The wine ultimately serves as a vehicle for festive times and great conversations, which explains why the heartbeat of Bent Creek is the tasting room and wine club. Pat Heineman shared the essence of the Bent Creek experience, "It's really about interacting with people and enjoying fine food and music in a festive atmosphere."

Every quarter they host a food and wine pairing for their wine club members. "The 200 to 250 club members that typically attend absolutely love our get-togethers," Carol says. "We even have one member, 'Bob the Grillmaster,' who fires up the barbie and tends the tri-tip all day long. His tri-tip acumen is so legendary he even has his own groupies!"

Pat and Carol say their goal is to provide visitors with an outstanding wine-tasting experience. "We offer our visitors a warm welcome and pleasant conversation as they taste our award-winning wines and picturesque vineyard views," they say. If you find yourself on the way to Bent Creek Winery, be sure to bring a picnic lunch and enjoy a bottle of their wine in the patio adjacent to the tasting room.

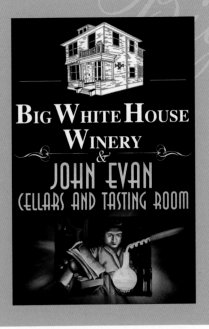

Big White House Winery
& John Evan Cellars
6800 Greenville Road
Livermore, CA 94550
(925) 449-1976

Website: www.bigwhitehouse.com
Email:
winemaker@bigwhitehouse.com

- Tasting room: weekends, noon–4:30, or by appointment;
  $5 tasting fee (waived with purchase)

- Established: 1998

- Owners/Winemakers: John Marion and John Evan Marion

- Annual production: 1,500 cases

- Varieties: Viognier, Roussanne, Marsanne, Chardonnay, Chenin
  Blanc, Sauvignon Blanc, Semillon, Mourvedre Rosé, Syrah Rosé,
  Petite Sirah, Syrah, Cabernet Sauvignon, Zinfandel, Pinot Noir,
  Mourvedre, Sangiovese, Carignane, Dolcetto, Malbec, Petite
  Verdot, late harvest Viognier, late harvest Syrah, fortified and
  botrytized Roussanne, and vintage and Tawny Port from Touriga
  Nacional, Tinta Cao, and Souzao

- Wine clubs: Friends of the Big White House and John Evan's
  Enomaniacs

- Original oil paintings of John Evan label art for sale
  (artists Laura and Diana Marion)

Fine wine, family, first-class food, art, and big fun

John "the Elder" Marion summed up his admiration for his son, John Evan, "When you become proficient at an art, the next thing you want to do is teach the art. There are some students with aptitude and some students who are spectacular, but then there's that one student who's remarkable, and in fact blows right by you and you can't teach him anything anymore—I'm lucky enough that my son is that person! Today, I'm the helper and my son is the winemaker."

It didn't start out that way. John Evan explained, "When my dad was making wine at home in 1992, I was a nine year old kid. There'd be thirty pounds of fruit in the bottom of a little garbage can and I could jump into the can a lot easier than the adults to stomp the grapes. That was my introduction!"

The family's winemaking adventures initiated when John Marion was employed as a research scientist at Livermore Labs. A yearlong stint in France in the mid-90s further propelled his passion for wine. Not long after returning to Livermore, Marion received a birthday gift of two oak barrels from a friend and

Photo courtesy of The Independent Magazine

Winemaker John Evan Marion in front of artwork that was used for some of his wine labels.

winemaker at Wente. That marked the beginning of the family's path to becoming professional winemakers.

"All of a sudden we were making barrels of wine instead of carboys," he remembers. Two years later, Marion's friend Earl Ault, owner of Cedar Mountain winery, offered to let them make wine in Ault's facilities.

Along the way, father and son took UC Davis extension courses, although Livermore Valley winemakers often proudly credit the critical tutelage received from industry professionals for transforming them from home winemakers into skilled artisans. "We are so indebted to Tom Lane at Concannon, Willie Joslin at Wente, and Earl Ault at Cedar Mountain for teaching us the technical winemaking skills and savoir faire," they say.

Marion says they are in the winemaking business to learn about wine. "We source from vineyards managed by growers who are extremely

View from inside the tasting room

Good times at Big White House and John Evan Cellars

Barrel tasting inside the winery

passionate about their vineyards, and we spend a lot of time in the vineyards with the growers because that's where the magic happens."

He describes their approach to winemaking as minimalist. They don't follow a formula for making their wines. Rather, each one is unique, guided by his son's intuition. "One of my son's talents is vision: being able to see, from a very early stage, where each wine is headed so he can tailor the process, from de-stemming through fermentation and aging to the choice of barrels."

The family launched the Big White House label in 1998 and have been making wine at their present location on Greenville Road since 2004. The ultra-luxury John Evan label was introduced on Evan's twenty-first birthday in 2005.

Crediting both of his parents, John Evan explains how he came to love the winemaker lifestyle, remembering art lessons from his mother and math quizzes from his father. "A winemaker is a blend of the artist and the scientist," he says.

Evan focuses primarily on single vineyard, single varietal wines. "I feel that the grapes have an idea of where they want to go, and I have an idea of where I want them to go. We kind of negotiate over the two-and-a-half to three years of aging, and you most often wind up with something much more interesting than when you blend."

The rustic, ranch-style tasting room is totally unpretentious, complete with wine aging in barrels. Striking oil paintings of John Evan label art by Laura and Diana Marion complement the special and unique atmosphere.

Father and son summed up the Big White House and John Evan Cellars experience: "It's all about fine wine, family, first-class food, art, and big fun."

BODEGAS AGUIRRE

2000
CABERNET SAUVIGNON

Livermore Valley
CALIFORNIA

Bodegas Aguirre Winery
8580 Tesla Road
Livermore, CA 94550
(925) 606-0554

Website:
www.bodegasaguirre.com
Email:
aguirre_sylvia@yahoo.com

- Tasting room: Weekends, noon–4:30;
  $5 tasting fee (waived with purchase)

- Established: 2001

- Owners: Dr. Ricardo (winemaker), and Margarita Aguirre

- Annual production: 2,300 cases

- Varieties: Cabernet Sauvignon, Merlot, Petite Sirah,
  Cabernet Franc, Malbec, Chardonnay, Pinot Noir,
  Zinfandel

- Wine clubs: Connoisseur and Elite wine clubs

Vino con Pasion

r. Ricardo Aguirre's family association with El Salvador coffee plantations created a lifelong fondness for the agrarian lifestyle, but his study of medicine brought him to America in 1969 to pursue a post-graduate career in cardiovascular surgery.

During his residency, Aguirre joined his attending physicians and fellow surgeons for periodic nights on the town, where he discovered and savored some of the finest wines from around the world. "During those days I developed a very sensitive palate and it continues to serve me well as a winemaker," he says. The Bordeaux classic Château Latour became his favorite. "At the time it sold for sixteen dollars a bottle!"

After completing his residency in 1976, Aguirre moved to California. During the past three decades, he practiced in Livermore and Danville, but with a demanding schedule of more than forty surgeries per month, he now limits his practice to Pleasanton. "Fortunately, I still have time for winemaking in the evenings and on weekends," he says, "and fortunately, it requires only my brains and taste buds, as I delegate the rest of the tasks."

Dr. Ricardo Aguirre, owner and winemaker of Bodegas Aguirre

For Aguirre, the path to becoming a winegrower and winemaker was a Sunday drive down the Tesla Road Wine Trail. He fell in love with the tranquility of Livermore Valley's vineyards. In 1989, Aguirre and his family became growers to supplement their income and purchased thirty-two acres next to Cedar Mountain Winery. In 1995, he planted twelve acres of Merlot and Cabernet Sauvignon, subsequently grafting a few rows over to Cabernet Franc. The following year, Aguirre purchased the current Bodegas Aguirre winery property, where he planted seven acres of Petite Sirah.

When the bottom fell out of the grape market in the late 90s, "rather than give the grapes to the birds," he made his first batch of home wine. Over the next two years, he produced half-barrels with the assistance of a professional winemaker. "But I couldn't legally put my name on a label," Aguirre recalls, "so I decided that if someone was going to make a mistake it should be me!" In 2002, their facility became a bonded winery, and Aguirre became the winemaker.

Through theoretical study, Aguirre says, he understood how most wineries in the world make their wine, and he boldly went from crafting a half-barrel to fifty-eight barrels the following year. "It was an amazing experience," he remembers. "The awards I was dreaming of for the future I received the very first year. Today, my goal is to remain at the forefront of winemaking in Livermore Valley." Recently, Aguirre's Petite Sirah won a "ten best" award for overall wines, while the Cabernet Sauvignon and Merlot were finalists.

Petite Sirah is Aguirre's flagship wine and biggest seller, followed by Cabernet Sauvignon, Merlot, Petit Verdot, Malbec, Cabernet Franc, and Syrah. To round out his offerings, he recently planted Tempranillo, Souzao, and Touriga Nacional, as well as a few Zinfandel vines. Aguirre offers fourteen reds and blends, along with a Chardonnay from Carneros. Castello Nuovo is Aguirre's proprietary blend of Merlot, Syrah, Petite Sirah, Cabernet Sauvignon, and Zinfandel. Reminiscent of a fine Rhone varietal, it was first crafted for his daughter's wedding but remains one of the winery's all-time favorites.

Aguirre also makes three different Ports. He crafted a special one for his first granddaughter and called it Victoria's Port in her honor. The namesake wine is Chardonnay-based with pear infused, aged Zinfandel Brandy. "It is just like going fishing," Aguirre says. "As soon as anyone tastes it, we just reel them in. I have yet to encounter anyone who does not want to buy it the moment they taste it."

Aguirre says he prefers the French winemaking style with extended maceration times. "With good exposure to new oak—most of our wines have eighteen months to two years in the barrel, with at least one year in the bottle. By definition all of our wines are reserve wines, and estate grown represents more than 90 percent of our total production."

For Bodegas Aguirre Winery and Vineyards, winemaking is a labor of love. "We do not expect to get rich in the process," Aguirre says. Specializing in estate-grown premium red wines, the family is proud to present the fruits of those labors that began fourteen years ago.

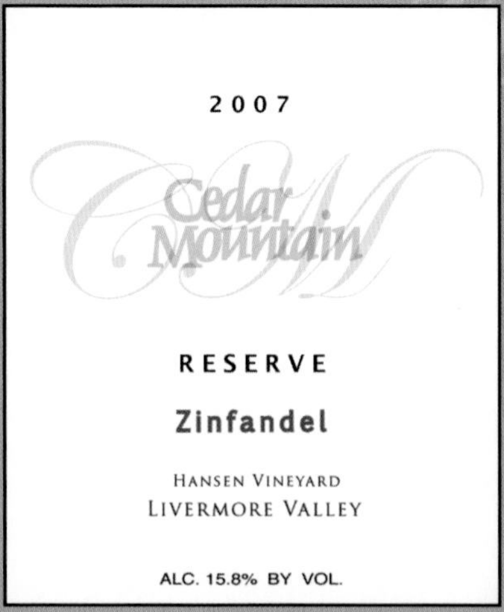

2007

Cedar Mountain

RESERVE

Zinfandel

HANSEN VINEYARD
LIVERMORE VALLEY

ALC. 15.8% BY VOL.

Cedar Mountain Winery
7000 Tesla Road
Livermore, CA 94550
(925) 373-6636

Website:
www.cedarmountainwinery.com
Email:
cedarmtn@wt.net

- Tasting room: Weekends, noon–4;
  $5 tasting fee (waived with purchase)

- Established: 1990

- Owners: Earl (winemaker) and Linda Ault

- Annual production: 22,000 cases (2,000 for Cedar
  Mountain and 20,000 for other Livermore wineries)

- Varieties: Estate Sauvignon Blanc, Estate Chardonnay,
  Estate Cabernet Sauvignon, Pinot Grigio, Viognier,
  Merlot, Syrah, Vintage Port, Viognier Port, and Port royale,
  Tortuga Royale (chocolate port), Zinfandel

- Wine club: Cedar Mountaineers

*Artistry Typifies the Valley's Only
Certified Green Winery*

*T*he tale of Linda and Earl Ault and their Cedar Mountain Winery is a trifecta of modesty, brilliance, and an inherent desire to help others find their way in the winemaking world.

Talk to a typical newcomer in the valley's winemaking community, and odds are the Aults will be mentioned with reverence. They are frequently credited with a litany of assistance, from crushing grapes, processing and bottling, and loaning a forklift or barrels to serving as winemaker-mentor.

Earl Ault's modesty revealed itself when he told me about his journey from novice to award-winning Port producer. In 1993, a neighbor told Ault about a grower in the Sierra Foothills who was willing to sell some Portuguese varietal grapes. "We bought a few tons and tried our luck making Ports," Ault remembers. "Imagine Larry, Curly, and Mo in the garage winery, sloshing alcohol into tubs of fermenting grapes with fumes wafting all over the place. I'm really surprised we didn't blow ourselves up!" Fortunately, Earl's Port turned out just fine, and he went on to craft a variety of distinctive, award-winning Portuguese varietals, barrel-aged for seven years. Today, the winery makes two white and three red Ports.

Linda Ault points out her husband's lack of pretense. "Earl's way too modest. A few years ago, *Wine Enthusiast* magazine named him one of the Top Five Port Producers in the entire United States." To this, Ault humbly counters, "Well, we're not big producers; we merely concentrate on quality."

The Aults began their winemaking journey in 1976. Living in eastern Washington, they were both working in energy—Earl as a physicist and Linda in physics and computer science. Fascinated by the budding local wine industry, the Aults joined the Northwest Enological Society. "That's when we started thinking about someday purchasing a vineyard," Linda remembers. They were transferred to the Livermore National Labs in 1981, and the valley's ideal growing conditions propelled their quest for a vineyard. Seven years later, the couple discovered a rare twenty-acre parcel planted with fourteen acres of Chenin Blanc. Six months after moving in, the Chenin Blanc was ready to harvest. That year they had a buyer, but the next year the buyer only wanted Cabernet and Chardonnay. "So we had the vineyard cut down and grafted over."

The Aults were content as growers until they noticed the superior characteristics of their new grapes. Holding back a few tons, they decided to make wine.

Concurrently, they learned everything they could about grape growing, vineyard management, and wine and brandy-making. Linda adds with a chuckle, "You name it, we've taken the course at UC Davis." And though the two jointly held six university degrees, they remember, "There we were back in school."

When the Aults began making Cabernet Sauvignon and Chardonnay in their

Cedar Mountain Winery

Linda and Earl Ault of
Cedar Mountain Winery

Estate Vineyards at Cedar Mountain Winery

three-car garage, they were the tenth Post-Prohibition winery to open in Livermore Valley. The Cabernet was released three years later, and it was an instant hit, earning three gold medals in national competitions. "Wine writers from all over were calling us up and asking, 'Who are you guys? Where did you come from?'" Earl recalls with a laugh, "And I'd reply, 'Kind of from nowhere!'"

Single varietals comprise the majority of Cedar Mountain's production, but the Duet, a blend of half Cabernet and half Merlot, outsells them all individually.

Presently, Cedar Mountain is the only green certified winery in Alameda County. The Aults have adhered to the Wine Institute's sustainable winegrowing practices since its inception around 2001, and their dedication has paid off.

The more I visited with the Aults, the more dimensions of their personalities unfolded. Sitting in Linda's kitchen, I commented on a culinary poster and she shyly shared her passion and background as a gourmet chef, which includes time studying in the company of Julia Child, Alice Waters, and Martha Stewart. Of course, she forgot to mention that she also attended the prestigious California Culinary Academy and that *Diablo* magazine named her one of the Five Best East San Francisco Bay Area Amateur Chefs. When I turned my gaze to their living room, I was awestruck by a series of large, dynamic, black-and-white prints that would easily blend in at the Chicago Art Museum. As Linda noticed my amazement, she said, "Oh, Earl shot those. He loves photography, too!"

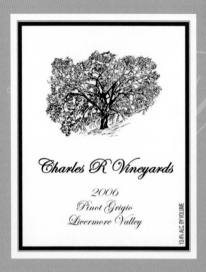

Charles R Vineyards
8195 Crane Ridge Road
Livermore, CA 94550
(925) 454-3040

Website:
www.charlesrvineyards.com
Email:
events@charlesrvineyards.com

- Tasting room: Friday–Sunday, noon–4:30; no tasting fee

- Established: 2002

- Owners: Dick and Bonnie Bartlett
  Winemaker: Randy Bartlett

- Annual production: 2,000 cases

- Varieties: Cabernet Sauvignon, Pinot Grigio, Chardonnay, Pinot Noir, Syrah, Zinfandel, and Port

- Wine clubs: Charles R Wine Club and The Miner's Club

Beyond the end,
where the grape experience begins.

*S*ometimes life takes interesting twists and turns. In the case of Charles Richard "Dick" Bartlett, a forty-year career as a professional excavator ultimately led to the creation of a premier boutique winery.

The seed germinated in 2002, when Dick and Bonnie Bartlett agreed to warehouse barrels and case goods for neighboring, family-owned wineries in their large barn and became a bonded wine facility.

Practically on a whim, their son, Randy, expressed his interest in winemaking and made a bold proposal to the family: that they open their own winery. Bonnie remembers, "We thought at the time that it would be such a simple process, but we quickly and painfully learned that the wine business is a very complex and time-devouring affair." Fortunately, the family loves the wine industry and enjoys meeting and getting to know the tasting room visitors and especially their wine club members. "They are like an extended family to us."

Randy serves as the winemaker, and his father is intimately involved in every detail. "It's a family affair," Randy says. "We named the winery Charles R after my father, and he often helps me in the cellar. He's my cellar rat and then some!"

Live music at Charles R Vineyards

If you visit the winery, you'll most likely see Charles zooming around on the forklift hauling barrels or racks, or working on one of his perpetual projects around the tasting room. He continues to manage their storage facility for other wineries and handles inventory control. "My husband is an amazing whirlwind worker bee," says Bonnie, who oversees the business side of the winery. "She's retired from the Livermore City Attorney's Office," Randy says, "but she works harder now than she did back then."

Randy's sister, Debra, a clinical nurse specialist, helps out in the tasting room whenever she can. Even Randy's son, Bailey, assists during harvest. He's operated the de-stemmer/crusher a few times and says he wants to be a winemaker when he grows up. Once, Randy recalls, he looked out the back door of the tasting room to find his son making s'mores for some of the guests. "The next thing I knew, Bailey was autographing wine bottles. He was twelve years old at the time!"

Winemaker Randy Bartlett checking barrels at Charles R Vineyards.

Award-winning hand-crafted wines

Like his mother who is a fine artist, Randy considers his wine-making to be an equally creative art form. For him, the real reward for his artistry happens in the tasting room. When people look up and smile as they sip his wine made from 100 percent Livermore Valley grapes, Randy says, "They'll talk about how much they enjoy my wine and ask if they can join our wine club…that's my priceless payback."

Randy's winemaking method is very traditional, and he uses American and French oak to intensify the various barrel characteristics. For example, he was aging a Pinot Noir in neutral French oak and it was not giving him any oak extractions, so he aged half in neutral oak and used new French oak for the remainder—and the wine worked out superbly. "The amazing thing was that with the addition of the new French oak, I only had to barrel age the Pinot Noir for twelve months," he recalls. "I normally have to go eighteen months with all my reds."

To achieve the ideal taste experience, Randy sometimes utilizes clone differentials. For his Zinfandel, he uses two clones. One is smoother with a big blackberry flavor, while the other imparts a spicy taste that gives a tingle across the tongue. Depending on how he barrel-blends, Randy can create a wine with all the spice up front and smoothing out toward the end; conversely, he can make it smooth up front with some spice at the finish. "Or in the case of the wine I am pouring right now," he explains, "it has spice all the way through, and people really enjoy that."

As you drive south on Greenville Road, the rural lane transmutes into Crane Ridge Road. And once you've rounded a bend just beyond the Big White House Winery, you'll probably think you've entered isolated ranching country and gone too far. That's precisely the moment when the Charles R Winery sign appears. The gravel entry lane dips past hillsides laden with massive oaks, and the rustic, architecturally inviting tasting room beckons you to picnic under the oaks and experience Charles R's award-winning, handcrafted wines.

2007
PASO ROBLES
MALBEC

ALCOHOL BY VOLUME 13.3%

Chouinard Vineyards
& Winery
33853 Palomares Road
Castro Valley, CA 94552
(510)-582-9900

Website: www.chouinard.com
Email: chouinard@chouinard.com

- Tasting room: Weekends, noon–5, or by appointment

- Established: vines planted 1978, winery opened 1985

- Owners: George, Caroline,
  and Damian Chouinard (winemaker)

- Annual production: 2,500 cases

- Varieties: Chardonnay, Viognier, Chenin Blanc, Gewürztraminer, Orange Muscat, Alicante Bouschet, Zinfandel,
  Cabernet Sauvignon, Petite Sirah, and Granny Smith Apple

- Wine club: VIT (Very Important Tasters) Club

Chouinard: A Petite Gem of a Vineyard

*C*houinard's encapsulating, bucolic, early-twentieth-century farm setting, nestled in the tree-shrouded Palomares Canyon, is an unforgettable destination—and it's an enticing reason why the winery also functions as a popular wedding venue and summer concert series locale where more than 200 people typically show up to enjoy everything from reggae to Cajun rock.

Before visiting Chouinard, I had heard about their multiple-award-winning Granny Smith apple wine, and it was a true "Wow!" moment to finally taste it. This fruit wine was so good that I would make a reprise visit to Chouinard just to taste and purchase more of this treat.

Some may turn up their noses at the mere mention of a fruit wine, but I assure you there's absolutely nothing sweet or syrupy about this incredible elixir. It's the next best thing to biting into the freshest and zestiest apple you've ever tasted. There's a

The tasting room at Chouinard Vineyards

cult following of Chouinard's apple wine, whose ardent fans return year after year to taste and purchase a case or two of this delectable treat. The fondness for their apple wine is so passionate it led the Chouinards to develop a cookbook featuring apple wine food pairings.

Equally tempting, their other offerings include an old vine Zinfandel, two delicious Cabernet Sauvignons, two Petite Sirahs, a killer Port, and an assortment of dessert wines that include an Orange Muscat, a sweet White Riesling, a fascinating ice-wine style Viognier, an old vine Zinfandel Port, and a Cabernet Port. They also produce an award-winning Methode Champenoise Champagne and a Charmot process sparkling wine. George and Caroline's son, Damian, is the winemaker. He learned the ABCs of fine winemaking at Fresno State's hands-on viticulture and enology program, along with an invaluable internship in the Champagne District of

Nestled in the East Bay foothills

Caroline and George Chouinard always welome guests at their wine variety of events.

Photo courtesy of The Independent Magazine

Estate vineyards

France. Damian's timing was spot on: his parents opened their winery in 1985, and he came on board as winemaker the following year. He's been there ever since. Chouinard wines are award-winning, and George and Caroline credit the technical expertise Damian developed in France.

In the 1987 Bay Area Competition (the very first contest they entered) Chouinard walked away with Best of Show for their Gewürztraminer. The same year, they won three silver medals at the Orange County Fair.

The Chouinards' ownership of the winery was prompted by George's desire to spend more time with his family. Trained as an architect, George spent most of his career in upper management of international engineering firms. In 1974, he was assigned to Paris as general manager of a large engineering and construction firm with projects across Europe and Africa.

Before going to France, the Chouinards already had a passion for wine and had tinkered with the idea of purchasing an existing Russian River winery but decided to put the temptation on hold. Then their two-year stint in France afforded them numerous opportunities to explore the world of French wines and wineries.

The Chouinards returned to America, but George felt unfulfilled on the road and away from his family. He decided to make a life change. "I had done so much international travel," he remembers, "and it was so disruptive to the family that I decided to return to the company I had worked for before, located in San Francisco." They purchased the 110-acre Palomares Road property in 1977 and started planting their vineyard in 1978. "This was our retirement project!"

In 1985, the Chouinard winery was bonded, and they opened their tasting room the same year. By all appearances, it was a brave but priceless decision to work close to home until retirement. Thirty plus years after settling in as growers and vintners, the family retains a close-knit relationship. They work, play, and live in close proximity to each other in the timeless Palomares Canyon.

Concannon Vineyard
4590 Tesla Road
Livermore, CA 94550
(925) 456-2505

Website:
www.concannonvineyard.com
Email:
info@concannonvineyard.com

- Tasting room: 11–4:30 daily; $5 tasting fee (includes keepsake glass)

- Established: 1883

- Owners: The Wine Group;
  Winemaker: Adam Richardson

- Annual production: 150,000 cases

- Petite Sirah, Merlot, Cabernet Sauvignon, Syrah, Grenache, Tempranillo, Chardonnay, Sauvignon Blanc, Pinot Gris, Pinot Noir, Zinfandel, Chardonnay, Viognier, and Rosé

- Wine club: Gatekeeper's Guild

America's First Petite Sirah

*W*inery Ambassador Jim Concannon says it best about his grandfather: "It was amazing that in 1865, this eighteen-year-old from Ireland's Aran Islands would daringly venture to a new country, raise a family of ten, and—knowing nothing about grapes or wine—establish a winery that's been an icon of Livermore Valley since 1883. Every time I think about it, all I can say is . . . wow!"

James Concannon sailed from Galway to New York, and after short stints working at the Singer Sewing Machine Company in Boston and as a bellhop in Maine, he ventured west and settled in San Francisco's Mission District—at the time a predominantly Irish-Catholic neighborhood.

Jim Concannon says his grandfather's close friendship with the city's first Catholic Archbishop, Joseph Alemany, was a transformational relationship. Alemany suggested that Concannon establish a winery to provide sacramental wine for the Catholic Church and recommended he consider a location in Livermore Valley, as the *terroir* was similar to Bordeaux and the Rhône Valley. Concannon purchased forty-seven acres in 1883 and built the winery in 1895. Today, his venture is revered as America's oldest Irish-American winery.

"Grandfather always sought out experts who knew more than he did," Concannon says. "He didn't just guess, and he seemed to quickly acquire knowledge in different fields." Following the advice of Charles Wetmore, a savvy neighboring vintner who introduced some of the first classic European varieties to Livermore Valley, James Concannon established his vineyard as a premier producer by sourcing the finest cuttings of Sauvignon Blanc and other legendary Bordeaux varietals from the famed Château d'Yquem in France, and planted the first Petite Sirah vines in 1906. Jim Concannon says, "Today our production also includes Cabernet Sauvignon and Merlot. Before the movie *Sideways* came out, we could barely give away our Pinot Noir—now it seems everybody wants it."

The Wine Group is the winery's corporate owner, but with third-generation Jim and fourth-generation John Concannon serving as national sales manager, the family maintains a gracious and welcoming presence at their ancestral family vineyard, which is listed on the California Register of Historical Landmarks.

If you mention the name Concannon to someone even vaguely familiar with the winery, they will probably ask if they're the ones who make the awesome Petite Sirah. They are, and it was Jim Concannon who introduced America's first varietally labeled Petite Sirah back in 1961. He explains, "The variety existed, but it was commonly known as Durif. We used to put it in our Burgundy." Following the suggestion of a Pasadena retailer, they produced wines labeled as Petite Sirah, and in less than four months the grocer sold out of the first shipment of 800 cases.

Historic entrance, built in 1935

Concannon's state-of-the-art solar-powered green winery

Rotary fermentor at Concannon Winery

It remains Concannon's flagship wine, and more than 140 of the winery's 200 acres in Livermore are planted with Petite Sirah vines grafted onto improved rootstock. Concannon's Estate Manager Jim Ryan notes that some of the vines are more than sixty years old. "They're the source of our Heritage label, which is produced exactly as the Concannons did years ago—with barrel aging up to three years or more," he says. Limited to about 200 cases per season, it's only produced when they have an exceptional year. Additionally, the vineyard limits their annual reserve wines to 1,000 cases per vintage.

Concannon is the world's second-largest producer of Petite Sirah, and Ryan says it's becoming an American favorite, with an annual growth rate of 17 percent.

Concannon introduced the widely utilized Cabernet Sauvignon Clones 7 and 11, and their Clone 8 is one of the most popular in California. Beginning as early as the 1970s, many of Napa's Cabernet vineyards were planted with Concannon's clones—and they still are. Another feather in their pioneering cap, Concannon was also one of the first California wineries to produce Bordeaux and Rhône-style wines.

Concannon's new barrel room is an impressive part of their newly opened state-of-the-art, 150-kilowatt, solar-powered, 43,000-square-foot facility. It holds about 4,000 barrels—in addition to the big, fifty-year-old French oak uprights, dubbed Concannon's "Petite Sirah Secret Weapon." Each one holds about 4,000 gallons, or roughly 1,400 cases, and they have replaced Concannon's late-nineteenth-century redwood tanks. Surprising to some, redwood barrels were commonly used by early California vintners.

Jim Concannon invites visitors to experience their beautifully designed new tasting room. "It's a work of art," he says. And while you're there, you might make a toast to their proud history of firsts—America's original Irish vintner who pioneered Bordeaux and Rhône-style wines in California and produced the country's first Petite Sirah is well worth lifting your glass to.

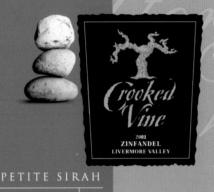

PETITE SIRAH

LIVERMORE VALLEY | 05

**Crooked Vine &
Stony Ridge Wineries
4948 Tesla Road
Livermore, CA 94550
(925) 449-0458**

Website: www.crookedvine.com
Email: info@crookedvine.com

- Tasting room: Monday–Saturday, 11–4:30; Sunday, noon–4:30; and by appointment; $5 tasting fee (waived with purchase)

- Established: Stony Ridge, 1975; Crooked Vine, 2002

- Owners: Rick and Pam Corbett
  Winemaker: Jamie Dowell

- Annual production: 5,000 cases

- Varieties: Cabernet Sauvignon, Merlot, Syrah, Petite Sirah, Zinfandel, Pinot Noir, Viognier, Fume Blanc, Chardonnay, Malvasia Bianca (still and sparkling)

- Wine clubs: Crooked Vine and Stony Ridge Wine Clubs

Estate-Grown Premium Wines

highlight of my visit to Crooked Vine and Stony Ridge Wineries was stepping through the rear doors of the tasting room to discover the Garden Terrace, a spacious and inviting shade-covered patio with ample greenery. Conjuring enticing visions of weddings, parties, and live music, this intimate outdoor space can accommodate up to 200 guests.

At the rear of the patio is the Barrel Room, which also serves as an indoor venue for dinner parties and receptions. There you'll find another special treat—two monstrous, eight-foot-tall oak wine barrels dating back to the 1850s. Created by Bavarian artisans and carried by ship around Cape Horn, the vessels are intricately hand-carved with bass relief vines and grapes. The Barrel Room can accommodate up to 100 guests.

Owners Rick and Pam Corbett, along with their son, Eric, started out in 1995 as growers when they planted twelve acres of Cabernet and Syrah on their Del Arroyo property in Livermore Valley. They continued to expand, and between 2000 and 2002 they planted an additional 150 acres of grapes.

A year eventually came along when they couldn't sell their harvest. But rather than panicking, the perpetual optimist Rick said to

Photo courtesy of *The Independent Magazine*

Winemaker Jamie Dowell and Eric Corbett

his son, "We can make wine! Let's go have some fun."

The family proceeded to harvest ten tons of Cabernet, ten of Syrah, and ten of Merlot. Before long, the Corbetts turned thirty tons of grapes into 2,000 cases of excellent red wine—but they had no way to sell it. Fortunately, not long after adding the second winery, Crooked Vine, the owner of Stony Ridge Winery offered to sell the facility to the Corbetts, under the same roof.

Rick Corbett proudly noted that their reds have won double Golds from the *San Francisco Chronicle*, and their Crooked Vine Syrah was recently awarded 98 points at the *Orange County Wine Competition*, while their Cabernet Sauvignon recently earned a Gold in the SF Chronicle Wine Competition as the best among 150 contenders in the $35 to $45 price range. Rick added, "Beating entries from Alexander Valley, Napa, and Sonoma. Of course we are very proud, especially since Eric and I grew the grapes ourselves."

Outdoor patio at Crooked Vine Winery

Eric Corbett of Crooked Vine and Stony Ridge Wineries

Photo courtesy of The Independent Magazine

Stony Ridge's new label design

All Crooked Vine and Stony Ridge wines are crafted from the Corbetts' estate-grown grapes. They annually process around 100 tons and sell 300 tons to six local wineries and three international concerns.

Jaime Dowell, Crooked Vine and Stony Ridge's young, vivacious winemaker, describes her craft as a melding of passions for art and wine. "I am not a painter, nor a sculptor, but I do consider myself an artist," she says.

For Dowell, a UC Davis graduate in viticulture and enology, winemaking is an opportunity to express her love for science and passion for creativity. "It's the only field in the world that allows me to express both sides simultaneously."

Dowell says she is delighted to work at a winery with 100 percent estate-grown grapes. "We are able to start our winemaking process in the fields. I work closely with our amazing vineyard manager, Juan Rios, who brings more than thirty years of experience to the table." When the grapes arrive at her cellar door, Dowell says, they're ready, and it's merely a matter of respecting the grapes' unique characteristics. "I taste in the field many times a week to determine the perfect moment to pick, and then it's time to start squishin'."

A strong believer in staying true to a varietal's natural tendencies, Dowell says Californians have steered toward big, bold, fruity wines. But she notes other varietals that are naturally more tannic, with a little bit of bite. "Those are beautiful qualities in wines such as Cabernet Franc and Cabernet Sauvignon. The real art of the winemaker shows in the blending process, along with knowing and respecting the varietals' natural characteristics. When you are able to harness what makes a grape unique and special on its own, you've allowed it to express its destiny!"

In addition to award-winning wines, Crooked Vine and Stony Ridge Wineries offer one of the most intimate settings in the Livermore Valley. "With beautifully landscaped grounds and the warm feel of our Barrel Room," Rick Corbett says, "our winery is the perfect venue for memorable special events."

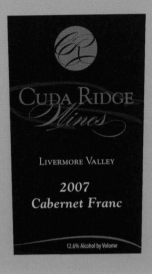

Cuda Ridge Wines
5385 East Avenue, Unit B
Livermore, CA 94550
(510) 304-0914

Website:
www.cudaridgewines.com
Email:
info@cudaridgewines.com
Facebook and Twitter

- Tasting room: Friday–Sunday, noon–4:30, or by appointment (check website for extended hours); minimal tasting fee for limited-production wines

- Established: 2007

- Owners: Larry and Margie Dino

- Annual production: 1,100 cases

- Varieties: Cabernet Sauvignon, Cabernet Franc, Merlot, Petit Verdot, Malbec, Sauvignon Blanc, and Semillon

- Wine club: Cuda Cadre

Bordeaux-Style Wines
with a California Twist

anta Clara native and registered nurse Margie Dino remembers the nearly two decades that she and her husband, Larry, made frequent wine-tasting trips to Napa and Sonoma. Then in 1999, they began making their own wine in their Fremont garage. That was the beginning of a hobby that, as Margie Dino says, "truly went wild."

Larry Dino, a software engineering director, recalls savoring the romance of the wine-country experience, "the aesthetics of the countryside, the excellent food and great discussions."

By the time the Dinos moved to Livermore in 2003, they were quite proficient in the art of winemaking, and their new custom home included a barrel room. "That's when my winemaking really kicked into high gear," Larry remembers. The Dinos got to know many of the farmers and vintners in the valley and decided to plant their own small vineyard with Cabernet Sauvignon and Merlot for their reserve.

Larry and Margie Dino

The couple continued to refine their winemaking skills, attending viticulture and enology courses through UC Davis and Las Positas Community College. By 2007, they were the proud owners of the bonded Cuda Ridge Winery.

I had been confident that Cuda Ridge winery was named in honor of some mountain range near their family's Italian ancestral homestead. But as I drove up to the tasting room, I realized the true namesake of the winery: Larry was tinkering with his "plum crazy purple" 1970 Barracuda muscle car. The plum-colored wine labels also pay homage to their fully restored "Cuda." Larry winked as he instructed me to look closely at the label, where I could just make out the suggestion of the car's lines in the understated brushstrokes.

Larry and Margie specialize in producing Bordeaux-style wines from a select group of Livermore Valley growers. Larry works closely with the growers to ensure an early harvest, which means that his grapes have lower sugar levels (typically 24–25 brix). Cuda Ridge blends its wines using Bordeaux varietals to produce old-world-style wines with an exceptional balance of fruit and earthy characteristics.

"We strive for a pleasant balance between fruit and the expression of Livermore Valley's *terroir* in the finished wines," he says. "Our wines are fruity but it's subtle, in the manner of an Italian or French wine."

Larry intentionally sources Livermore Valley grapes because he believes they are outstanding. "We are dedicated to providing handcrafted, limited-production wines with complexity and layers that reflect the distinctive characteristics of old-world, Bordeaux-style wines—with a California twist." Cuda Ridge's marriage of new French oak with American oak, Larry points out, is what creates that twist.

Cuda Ridge wines are generally blends of classic Bordeaux varietals and are crushed, pressed, and barrel aged at the winery in small lots. They describe their wines as a true labor of love, produced in lots of 50 to 200 cases by family and friends.

Pay a visit to the tasting room, and you are bound to meet one of the Cuda Ridge owners or friends who produce these exceptional wines. You may even catch a glimpse of a classic muscle car or see the winemaking in process.

Outside Cuda Ridge Winery

Darcie Kent Vineyards & Underdog Wine Bar
4590 Tesla Road
Livermore, CA 94550
(925) 456-2505

Website:
www.darciekentvineyards.com
Email:
Darcie@darciekentvineyards.com

- ℂℓ Tasting room/wine bar: noon–8; current releases sold by 2 oz. taste or 6 oz. glass
- ℂℓ Established: 1996
- ℂℓ Owners: David and Darcie Kent, The Wine Group LLC
- ℂℓ Winemaker: Julian Halasz
- ℂℓ Annual production: 10,000 cases
- ℂℓ Varieties: DeMayo Chardonnay and Zinfandel, Picazo Vineyard Merlot, West Pinnacles Chardonnay and Pinot Noir, Madden Ranch Cabernet Sauvignon, Rava Blackjack Sauvignon Blanc and Grüner Veltliner, and Crown Block Merlot

Where the Palette Meets the Palate

*D*arcie Kent is a fourth-generation vintner. Her great grandfather, Christian Ruegsegger, emigrated from Switzerland in 1875 and founded his Alpine Winery in St. Joseph, Missouri. Its bond number was 62. To give you an idea of how low a number that is (and therefore how early an operation it was), Livermore's oldest winery, Concannon Vineyard, holds bond number 616. The area's newest winery, Nottingham Cellars, holds bond number 16533.

Just like her great grandfather, Darcie Kent is an acclaimed artist, and her creative sensibilities are expressed in her wine endeavors. "I look at vineyards with an artist's eye," she says.

Darcie Kent wines are handcrafted, limited-production, single-vineyard bottlings. "Every vineyard reflects the personality of its owner," she believes, "and so will the wine." Kent is inspired by dynamic, vibrant landscapes, and she strives to translate this intensity to her canvases and her wines. "These vineyards, like their owners, are complex and possess a graceful elegance," she says. "I try to capture this with paint and with wine so we can savor them together."

Not surprisingly, Kent has created a painting of each vineyard to adorn her labels. The label for Madden Ranch Cabernet Sauvignon is "bold and fired-up" just like the vineyard's owner, football legend John Madden. The label she created for another Livermore Valley vineyard, owned by Frank and Heidi DeMayo, is "intense and straightforward." The vibrant labels communicate a sense of place for each wine and echo her large landscape paintings that are part of private and public collections throughout the world.

Many Darcie Kent wines are crafted in extremely small lots, often less than ten barrels. These wines sell out quickly but can still be found on better wine lists throughout the Tri-Valley region. And Kent has recently diversified her offerings. Rather than exclusively producing heavy, long-lived reds, she now focuses on another passion: aromatic white wines.

She is especially interested in a rare, California-grown Grüner Veltliner—the great Alpine grape of Austria. "With my focus on producing great food wines that really complement a meal," she explains, "I was drawn to a unique site in Monterey—the Rava Blackjack vineyard—which specializes in many lesser known grape varieties grown with bright acidity and pure fruit flavors."

In the winemaking process, she is elated to be working with Hungarian-born Julian Halasz of Concannon. At harvest time, she describes him as a grape-ivore who walks each vineyard munching entire grape clusters. Not relying on the numbers, he can taste when the fruit is at its peak of ripeness, knowing the flavors will be perfectly translated into wine. "When everything is absolutely perfect, we'll pick that night."

Darcie Kent wines are available at The Underdog Wine Bar located inside the recently restored Concannon Hospitality Center. It is a spacious and hip lounge-style venue where local and global winemakers are regularly featured. When weather permits, wines can be enjoyed *al fresco* under a lovely arbor.

Not all Underdog wines have small production and limited availability.

Several brands, such as Cupcake Vineyards, Big House, and BoHo, make extensive use of locally grown Livermore Valley grapes in addition to fruit grown all along the central Coast. Of special note are the Mediterranean-style wines offered under these labels, especially the Petite Sirah, Grenache, Malbec, Zinfandel, and Syrah.

The Underdog Wine Bar also features a kennel full of imported, family-owned wineries. Most notable are Helfrich (Alsace, France), Chockstone (Melbourne, Australia), Kallfelz (Mosel, Germany), Montecillo (Rioja, Spain), and Albino Armani (Trento, Italy). All wines are available to taste and amazingly fresh, thanks to the largest nitrogen bar system in the Tri-Valley area—an Italian-built, forty-eight-bottle, temperature-controlled installation that stretches across the entire length of the back bar.

A good way to explore this extensive offering of unique, often undiscovered wines is to select a flight of three 2-oz. pours. They can be from a single producer, a single region, or a single grape variety, which allows you to compare and contrast without consuming too much. Guest winemakers are a regular draw to Underdog, and the experience is greatly enhanced by the knowledgeable staff and their broad offering of international flatbread pizzas, which are carefully paired to complement each flight of wine.

The Web-based Underdog Wine Merchants was created in 2005 to offer emerging wine brands with unique appeal to young adult consumers—in particular the millennial generation. Many of the wineries are small, California-family-owned producers, such as Mutt Lynch, a Dry Creek Valley Zinfandel boutique, and Brophy Clark, a Santa Barbara Pinot Noir specialist.

Given the renaissance of winemaking in the Livermore Valley, it is refreshing to see how dedicated local vintners such as Darcie Kent are taking a seat at the global table and proudly pouring their wines alongside the best that the world has to offer.

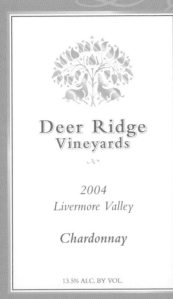

Deer Ridge
Vineyards
℘

2004
Livermore Valley

Chardonnay

13.5% ALC. BY VOL.

Deer Ridge Vineyards
1828 Wetmore Road
Livermore, CA 94550
(925) 743-9427

Website:
www.DeerRidgeVineyards.com
Email:
info@DeerRidgeVineyards.com

- Tasting room: Thursday–Sunday, 11–5, and by appointment; $5 fee for reserved flight, others complimentary

- Established: 2000

- Owners: Cherie and Carl Lyle

- Annual production: 5,000 cases

- Varieties: Chardonnay, Cabernet Sauvignon, Petite Sirah, Syrah, Zinfandel, Tempranillo, Barbera, Pinot Noir, Sauvignon Blanc, Viognier, Syrah Rosé, Sangiovese, Merlot, Port, and sparkling wine

- Wine club: Deer Ridge Vineyards Wine Club

A Winery Estate and Gathering Place

ack in the 1880s, Livermore pioneer wine grower Clarence Wetmore grew grapes for his brother's legendary Cresta Blanca Winery on the land that is now home to Deer Ridge Vineyards. Cherie and Carl Lyle continue the Wetmore legacy by nurturing their twenty-six acres of award-winning grapes. But today, there's a lot more than grape growing happening at Deer Ridge.

In 2007, the Lyles opened their stunning, Tuscan-style, multi-purpose winery and event center. The foyer greets you with a welcoming air that deftly blends the warmth of an opulent home with sophisticated, modern technology. The artful design is inspired by Carl's previous corporate incarnation as an operations manager charged with high-tech facility construction and renovation. Museum-quality art graces the walls throughout, and a professional curator selects and periodically rotates the pieces.

In addition to serving a discerning wine-tasting crowd, Deer Ridge specializes in corporate events and parties, holiday gatherings, and, most notably, wedding ceremonies and receptions.

Photo courtesy of The Independent Magazine

Cherie and Carl Lyle of Deer Ridge Vineyards

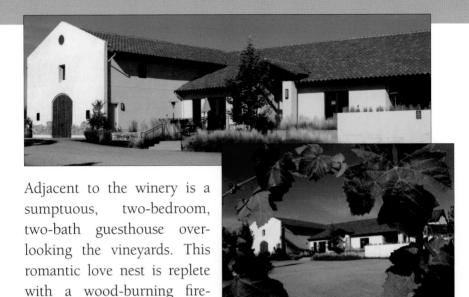

Deer Ridge Vineyards

Adjacent to the winery is a sumptuous, two-bedroom, two-bath guesthouse over-looking the vineyards. This romantic love nest is replete with a wood-burning fire-place, opulent gourmet kitch-en, soaking tub, and private patio with a fire pit. It's often booked in conjunction with weddings but is just as popular with couples seeking over-the-top wine weekend getaways.

The Lyles also offer gourmet onsite catering services with a din-ing room that seats up to 128 people and a barrel room that's used for intimate dining, wedding ceremonies, and rehearsal dinners.

Even without the event center, Deer Ridge would remain a must-see destination for a taste of award-winning wines. Be sure to ask for their signature Moonstruck meritage. As Carl explained, they harvest the grapes at night under a full moon, "partially for the romance of it, but also because it's fun." The Moonstruck event is held in conjunction with a winemaker dinner, and guests help harvest the grapes by torchlight. Participants are responsible for approximately one barrel, and throughout the aging process they return to sample their harvest. When the wine is released, they each receive a free bottle of the finished Moonstruck blend.

When a friend double dared them to prove they could make truly exceptional banquet wine, Carl and Cherie took the challenge. The result? An amazing banquet wine from their estate 2004 Cabernet Sauvignon that won Gold, Best of Class, and a 4-Star Gold among

3,200 contenders in the Orange County Wine Competition. "We were delighted with the recognition," they say. "It proved that our vineyards are capable of producing world-class wine."

To position Deer Ridge wines in the minds of consumers, Cherie says they have followed the maxim "labels on tables." They also offer fifteen wines for under fifteen dollars and try to keep even their finest bottles under thirty dollars—products that are comparable to those ranging in the fifty to one hundred dollar range coming out of Napa and Sonoma Valleys. "Our award-winning Cab proves it," the couple says, "because it beat out one hundred dollar Napa Cabs in subsequent blind tasting events." Deer Ridge also produces superb whites. For example, their 2007 Chardonnay Reserve was awarded a gold medal in the Best of the Bay competition.

The Lyles became growers and producers in 1992 when Carl—with zero winemaking experience at the time—tried his hand as the official blender in a home winemaking venture with a buddy. When the two entered a competition at St. Supéry winery in Napa, Carl remembers, "We won Best of Class, Best of Show, and Best Cab, and I've never looked back since."

After this auspicious beginning, a mid-life shift in priorities prompted them to leave corporate life and search from Mexico to Canada for the perfect winery location. While exploring Livermore Valley, Carl and Cherie presented their business plan to Phil Wente, who directed them to the old Wetmore Ranch property. As they say, the rest is history.

When I asked about the name Deer Ridge, Cherie, a master gardener, explained that the half-acre surrounding her Danville home was planted with a profusion of greenery, including grapevines. "The deer were so fond of my creations that we named our homestead Deer Ridge, and thus, the namesake of our winery and label."

Eagle Ridge Vineyard
10017 Tesla Road
Livermore, CA 94550
(925) 447-4328

Website:
www.eagleridgevineyard.com
Email: eagleridgevnyd@aol.com

- Tasting room: Saturday and Sunday, noon–4:30, and by appointment
- Established: 2003
- Owners: Jim and Cheryl Perry
- Winemaker: Earl Ault; winemaker-in-training: Jim Perry
- Annual production: 1,000 cases
- Varieties: Pinot Grigio, Petite Sirah, Zinfandel, Cabernet Sauvignon, and Madlyn (dessert wine)
- Wine club: Taste of the Vines Wine Club

Livermore Owned, Livermore Grown

*I*t all began with weeds. Jim and Cheryl Perry were living at the current Page Mill Winery location, and they dreaded the unending chore of weed-eating their 2.8 acres. A friend asked, "Why not plant a vineyard? It's really simple, and there's no maintenance."

The Perrys liked the idea, so in 2003 they planted two acres of Petite Sirah. A few years later, they found themselves harvesting four tons of grapes, and they couldn't give nearly enough away to their friends. So with no previous experience beyond two decades of weekend wine tasting jaunts to Napa and Sonoma wineries, the couple started making wine and simultaneously enrolled in viticulture, enology, vineyard maintenance, and chemistry courses through UC Davis and the local community college.

Cheryl, a Livermore native who grew up on the backside of Concannon Winery, says she has always associated autumn with must and fermentation. Sometimes she's amazed they did not get into the wine business sooner. Jim, a Missouri native, moved to Livermore in 1957 and entered law enforcement. Since 1983, he's worked as an appraiser and realtor.

As the couple ventured forth, Cheryl says, "We had no idea that the winemaking process would be highly complex. It is so far beyond complex that it's amazing." Fortunately, Cheryl's training as a registered nurse provided her with a functional comprehension of the requisite chemistry.

The Perrys were also blessed with two brilliant mentors who helped them immensely as they started out: Earl and Linda Ault of Cedar Mountain Winery. "To this day they do our crushing, bottling, and lab work," Cheryl says. "We were below novice in the beginning and the other winery owners were so helpful. People came forward and asked how they could help. It's just been phenomenal! Earl Ault remains our expert winemaker, and I suspect that we will remain winemakers-in-training until we die!"

In 2005, the Perrys moved to a larger property with an existing half-acre of Cabernet and immediately planted Petite Sirah, Zinfandel, and Pinot Grigio. They brought in their first harvest in 2009. Proud enthusiasts of Livermore Valley's superb grapes, Jim says, "We don't believe that people come all the way out here to taste wines made from San Diego, Napa, Sonoma, or Lodi grapes. They want to discover Livermore Valley wines."

The Eagle Ridge tasting room is an unpretentious space in the front quarter of the barrel storage facility. Visitors love walking around and looking at their eclectic antique treasures, as well as reading the varietal tags on the barrels. "We are a family-oriented winery, and we want every aspect of our visitors' experience to be comfortable and casual," Cheryl says proudly. As the grandparents to two young granddaughters, they are well aware that many young couples with children

Photo courtesy of *The Independent Magazine*

Award-winning wines at Eagle Ridge Vineyards

Tasting bar at Eagle Ridge Vineyards

want to go wine tasting. "We encourage them to bring their kids along. We even have blackboards, toys, and a play area outside."

The Perrys have no interest in becoming a volume producer and are comfortable limiting production to no more than 1,200 cases per year. "We want small lots with everything focused on the grapes," Cheryl says. "We don't do a lot of barrel blending or overwork the grapes. We concentrate on showing what the very best of a particular varietal can be." Nearly all (90 percent) of their wine is aged in French oak, with 25 percent in neutral barrels, 50 percent in one- to five-year-old barrels, and 25 percent in new barrels. Eagle Ridge wines are barrel aged from thirty to thirty-six months.

The Perrys have a small advertising budget and benefit from the local vintners' community spirit of referrals. That is Eagle Ridge's primary source for first-time visitors, and, Cheryl says, it's invaluable because tasting room purchases account for 95 percent of their sales. Jim notes that the Livermore Valley Wine Growers Association is another invaluable resource, along with their participation in civic events and non-profit fundraisers.

One of their first non-grape projects at the new property was to become Livermore Valley's first winery to be powered entirely by solar energy. The Perrys' 10 kilowatt array now energizes the entire winery operation, outbuildings, residence, swimming pool, and spa. And they even sell back to the grid when they produce excess.

Eckert Estate Winery
2400 Arroyo Road
Livermore, CA 94550
(925) 371-8606

Website:
www.eckertestate.com

- Tasting room: Saturday and Sunday, noon–5, and by appointment; $3 fee per person for groups of eight or more

- Established: 2001

- Owners: Michael (winemaker) and Vickie Eckert

- Annual production: 2,000 cases

- Varieties: Viognier, Semillon, Verdelho, Cabernet Sauvignon, Malbec, Zinfandel, Petite Sirah, Syrah, Dolcetto, Mourvedre, Trincadiera, Tempranillo, Merlot, Touriga Nacional, Alvarelhão, Carignane, Charbono, and Primitivo. Blends: Ensemble (Cabernet, Carignane, Syrah, Petite Sirah, and Zinfandel), Mistura della Campagna (field blend of nine Italian varieties), Boa Quinta Mistura (five Portuguese varieties), Classic Meritage (Cabernet Sauvignon, Merlot, and Malbec), Portuguese-style five-grape Port, and Reunion Port (Syrah and Petite Sirah)

- Wine club: Insiders Wine Club

We dare you to find us!

*I*n 1985, Michael and Vickie Eckert purchased a few acres in Livermore, assuming they'd be content with equine activities. Little did they know that a winemaker dinner at Wente's restaurant would radically change their lives. Industry legends Bob and Gloria Taylor of Retzlaff Winery turned out to be their randomly selected tablemates, and they asked the young couple what their plans were for their acreage. "Horses?" Bob puzzled, "You should plant grapes!" The Eckerts agreed and subsequently planted one hundred of the Taylors' pruned canes, followed by another hundred Petite Sirah cuttings from Concannon, and then some Mourvedre from Thomas Coyne. They were hooked.

Michael signed up for every UC Davis vitacultural extension course available and continued to receive invaluable mentorship from Thomas Coyne and Lanny Replogle of Fenestra Winery. It was at Fenestra that Eckert made his first wine while serving an eighteen-month cellar-rat apprenticeship under Replogle.

Eckert Estate

Eckert was the twentieth winery to open in Livermore, and right out of the chute their Petite Sirah won a gold medal and Best of Region at the California State Fair. "At the time, I thought we'd hang our hat on that," Michael says. "But today, Malbec is the wine we are closely associated with, partly because we were among the first in the valley to produce it va-

Wines at Eckert Estate

rietally." Eckert's Estate Cabernet Sauvignon is their most coveted wine, while their Port recently won a Four Star Gold Medal from the Orange County Wine Competition. Eckert's guiding light is quality, along with affordability, and he tries to keep all of his wines priced under $20. "The price of a bottle of wine should be determined by the cost of making it plus a reasonable profit," he says. "Way too many wines today are over-priced and are testing what the market will bear. I emphasize real value, not perception of value."

Eckert works in the tasting room at least one day each week-end to keep in tune with how customers are receiving his wines and to discern what they are looking for. He says that his most well-received wine has been his Ensemble blend. Consulting with Lanny Replogle, Eckert blended a 50/50 Cab and Carignane mix. To spice it up they added some Petite Sirah, Syrah, and Zin, and wound up with an awesome red table wine. It sells for around $10 a bottle.

Eckert primarily produces small lots, and the majority of his non-mainstream varietals are less than six barrels (at approximate-ly twenty-five cases per barrel). "I enjoy having the flexibility to explore new varieties, and my customers enjoy being introduced to wines they can't find in stores," he says. Eckert barrel ages in French and American oak, and ages his red wines longer than most wineries (three to four years on average). "When I release a wine, it is ready to drink and be enjoyed. That said, many of my wines have additional aging potential, but it's not a necessity."

Eckert's real passion is blending. "I love to do blendings, and I like to work with a variety of wines because it gives me a full palette to paint with. We have always prided ourselves on being a little off the mainstream. We love to put wines out like Charbono and Dolcetto, Touriga Nacional, and Verdelho."

Even though most of his wines are not necessarily advertised as blends, it's rare that Eckert releases a wine from a single variety. Most single-grape wines are not naturally in perfect balance, he says. "When blending a varietal release, I strive to maintain varietal character while balancing nose, front-palate, and mid-palate, and finish with the addition of complementary wines." Blending is an art, he says, one that requires a cellar with numerous wine options. "By having many wines and several vintages available in my cellar, I have a large array of tools with which to blend."

The view from Eckert's unpretentious tasting room is framed by olive trees, vines, and surrounding hills, and the active wildlife go about their business undisturbed by the winery's presence.

The Eckerts hope that when people visit their tasting room, "they will walk away having tried at least one wine that is a totally new experience." Given their bountiful, award-winning selection to choose from, that seems like a goal well within reach.

el sol Winery
8626 Lupin Way
Livermore, CA 94550
(925) 606-1827

Website: www.elsolwine.com
Email: hal@elsolwine.com

- Tasting room: Friday–Sunday, noon–5, and by appointment; $5 fee for el Sol Wine, $10 fee for Reserve Wine

- Established: 2002

- Owners: Kathy and Hal (winemaker) Liske

- Annual production: 4,000 cases

- Varieties: Zinfandel, estate-grown Syrah, Barbera, Charbono, Mourvedre, Tempranillo, Cabernet Sauvignon, Merlot, Sangiovese, Viognier, Chardonnay, Pinot Grigio, Lodi Primitivo, late-harvest Sauvignon Blanc, Tawny Port, Grand Cuvee Champagne, and Muscat

- Wine club: Solstice Wine Club

Wines Made with Skill, Passion, and the Spirit of el Sol

*I*n 1997, as Captain Hal Liske was approaching the end of his thirty-six-year career with the Hayward Fire Department, he purchased an abandoned Foster Farms chicken ranch on the outskirts of Livermore. At the time, he thought he'd comfortably grow old operating a honey business. But, as he describes it, his passion for making homemade wine went "totally haywire!"

Liske's detour into the wine business began when a friend gave him some grapes as a gift. At the time, his wife, Kathy, was working at Stony Ridge Winery. Hal remembers that her coworkers tutored her husband in the fundamentals of winemaking and that she received invaluable technical assistance from Tim Sauer of Livermore Valley Cellars.

Liske entered into a custom-crush contract with Garré Winery until fall 2003, when his el Sol facility was formally bonded and licensed. He converted some of the old Foster Farm structures into a tasting room, processing area, and barrel facilities. "We've been making wine here ever since," he says, "and not only for ourselves. We offer custom-crush services for our customers, as well."

One of his specialties is winemaking for people who have grapes in their back yards but no processing facilities. "A lot of our clients have the ability to make their own wine," Liske explains. "But especially with red wines, they do not have the space to store them for three or four years, so we also provide barrel storage services." Liske keeps a close eye on his customers' product and tops up the barrels as needed.

The Liskes grow a small amount of their own grapes, including Zinfandel and Syrah, but the majority are sourced from growers in Livermore Valley and nearby Lodi, Amador, and Contra Costa Counties.

Typically barrel aging his reds for four years, Liske counsels his storage customers to do the same. "I believe the wait is well worth it, and I think that a central reason why my wines are well received is that they are all fully matured, table ready, and consumer friendly upon release."

el Sol offers a few austere, European-style wines, but for the most part the reds are big, fat, and very jammy. Because he also ages his white wines longer than most wineries, they express divergent and yet enticing characteristics. His Sauvignon Blanc, Viognier, and Pinot Gris, for example, are all a little more on the buttery side, are a little rounder and smoother, and have a subtle vanilla kick.

Liske's winemaking style rests on the firm belief that the oak's job is to push the fruit forward. "I use 95 percent once-used French oak, and I like the fact that my red wines spend maximum time in the barrel without getting over-oaky—after all, we are not selling oak flavor, we're selling grape flavor!"

Tasting tables provide a casual ambiance at el Sol Winery.

The tasting bar at el Sol

Inside the tasting room at el Sol

"In our grape processing, everything we do gets sorted. We'll run the de-stemmer real slow and when the fruit comes out the bottom someone will be down there picking out the stems, so our ferments are very clean." "When the berries drop out of the de-stemmer, rather than going into a crusher they go directly into the fermentation bins." Nearly 90 percent of el Sol's wine production is done in whole berry fermentation.

Liske enjoys the benefits of his facility's location on the fringe of the wine trail footprint. "It saves us from the limo crowd and those just seeking a convenient place to get toasted. The people who show up at our door are often referred by our regular customers." And referral, Liske believes, is the ideal business model.

Wine is only part of the equation in el Sol's tasting room sales. Good memories of a tasting-room experience, Liske says, are often based on the interactions and conversations with the winemaker or tasting room attendant. "The wines are often purchased as a memento of a great afternoon," he says.

The couple designed their tasting room around a café tabletop layout to facilitate friendlier interactions between the staff and customers. Liske believes the typical tasting room bar serves as a barrier between staff and guests. "We also subscribe to the Nordstrom model, so within three seconds of entering the tasting room our guests are welcomed and we introduce ourselves with a first name." Above all, Liske says, the goal at el Sol Winery is to make good food-and-party-wine that people will truly enjoy.

Elliston Vineyards
463 Kilkare Road
Sunol, CA 94586
(925) 862-2377

Website: www.elliston.com
Email: info@elliston.com
Facebook

- Tasting room: weekends, 11–5; weekdays, by appointment
- Established: 1890, Elliston; 1982, winery
- Owner/Winemaker: Donna Awtrey Flavetta
- Annual production: 3,000–5,000 cases
- Varieties: Cabernet Sauvignon, Cabernet Franc, Merlot, Pinot Blanc, Pinot Gris, Chardonnay, Pinot Noir, Danse de Blanc, Captain's, and Sparkling wine
- Wine club: Club 200

Taste the History

Sometimes a winery's story has as much to do with the incredible setting as it does with the wines. In Elliston's case, it's a toss up. The historic Elliston mansion is breathtakingly beautiful, while their excellent red wines are sometimes aged in the barrel for up to three to four years and bottle aged for the same.

Elliston also offers an onsite restaurant, a corporate retreat center, and a popular wedding venue. A visit there is a seductive environmental and architectural experience—odds are that you'll fall in love with the lushly foliated setting and depart with reluctance, as I did.

The winery's enchanting centerpiece is the stately, blue, sandstone three-story mansion. Listed on the National Register of Historic Places, the home is clad in sandstone that was quarried in nearby Niles Canyon and boasts stone arches and walls nearly three feet thick. The structure and surroundings are remarkably unchanged from the day the Ellis family took residence in their freshly completed home in 1890.

In 1885, former San Francisco Police Chief and grain merchant Henry Ellis (the namesake of San Francisco's Ellis Street)

Beautiful landscaping at the Mansion at Elliston Vineyards

commenced construction of the seventeen-room, three-story estate, sequestered in a sleepy canyon on the outskirts of the farming and ranching community of Sunol. Five years later, Ellis planted three acres of grapes. It was a time when the entire Sunol region burgeoned with new wineries. By 1898, there were fourteen vineyards in Sunol, collectively harvesting 148 acres of mostly European varietals.

The Mansion in Sunol Valley

During the first half of the twentieth century, the Elliston property went through numerous owners until 1969, when Ramon and Amy Awtrey purchased the estate. Their daughter, Donna Flavetta, was seven years old when they moved in. She still lives there today along with her children and grandchildren,

Ciera, Jenni, and Mark Piche at Elliston

who are actively involved in the day-to-day operations.

When the Awtrey family started their winery operation, they also took over management of fifty-five acres of the nearby Sunol Valley Vineyards and planted three acres of Chardonnay grapes on their estate. Flavetta remembers that when her parents started bottling in 1982, there were only seven or so wineries in the entire Livermore Valley.

She purchased the winery from her parents in 1992 when they retired and moved back to her mom's hometown on Kauai. Five generations of Awtrey Flavetta's family have grown up on the property, and today, her son, Mark, serves as vice president of operations.

Flavetta notes, "We have always known that Livermore Valley produces exceptional fruit, and staying local allows us to work closely with the grower."

Flavetta is an ardent believer in not releasing a wine until it's fully aged. "We cellar our wines a minimum of two years and up to ten years before release. The wines we sell are true library wines. When you buy a wine from Elliston, it's ready to enjoy."

In addition to single varietals, Elliston produces both red and white blends. Their red blend, Captain's Claret, has become the vineyard's signature wine. It's a blend of 70 percent Merlot, 19 percent Cabernet Franc, and 11 percent Cabernet Sauvignon. Flavetta's parents were the first in the region to produce Pinot Gris in 1982, and it remains one of their most popular wines.

The Elliston tasting room is located inside the mansion, and the 2,000-square-foot Terrace Room is just a few steps away. The Terrace Room and adjoining outdoor patio (which can accommodate up to 225 guests) serve as versatile spaces for meetings, receptions, and indoor weddings. But by far, the choicest spot to tie the knot at Elliston is under the sprawling oak trees, the majestic stone mansion serving as a romantic backdrop. Elliston also specializes in themed events, including murder mystery evenings, cooking classes, and reunions, as well as tea parties and baby showers.

For an attractive and unique alternative to traditional meeting facilities, visit the beautifully landscaped grounds of Elliston Vineyards. And as Donna Flavetta says, "Elegance, style, and grace mark every aspect of the Elliston Vineyard experience." I can't disagree.

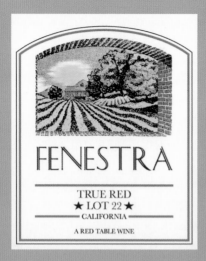

Fenestra Winery
83 Vallecitos Road
Livermore, CA 94550
(925) 447-5246

Website:
www.fenestrawinery.com
Email:
info@fenestrawinery.com

- Tasting room: Friday–Sunday, noon–5;
  $5 tasting fee (waived with purchase)

- Established: 1976

- Owners: Fran and Lanny Replogle
  Winemaker: Brent Amos

- Annual production: 8,000 cases

- Varieties: Verdelho, Sauvignon Blanc, Semillon, Semonnay,
  Chardonnay, Viognier, White Riesling, Pinot Noir, True Red,
  Merlot, Alvarelhão, Touriga, Cabernet Sauvignon, Mourvedre,
  Syrah, Tempranillo, Cabernet Franc, Zinfandel, Petite Sirah,
  Sweet Viognier, Port

- Wine club: Fenestra Fanatics

Award-winning wines in a
friendly, historic setting

A visit to Fenestra Winery is like traveling back in time to 1889, when the property was first developed as a vineyard and wine-processing facility by Livermore Valley pioneer George True.

Inside the ancient, redwood-clad winery, you'll see heavy timber beams and thick vintage-plaster walls. You might even feel the palpable sense of those who trod through the winery a century ago.

George True produced bulk wine, and as far as the Replogles know, he did not bottle any of his own product but shipped it in tank cars to San Francisco, the Midwest, and New York. Sadly, True died at a young age in 1896, and his wife, Christina, took over operations.

Prohibition corked the sale of True's bulk wine. After Prohibition, a nephew took over and sold off the stockpiled wines under the Golden Rule Winery & Vineyard label.

When the Replogles founded Fenestra in 1976, the old winery was abandoned and literally on the verge of collapse. A massive structural renovation regenerated the facility for another hundred years of service. Fortunately, they left the ancient bones of the main barn-like structure exposed.

The Replogles' road to stewardship of one of Livermore Valley's few remaining pioneer wineries began during Lanny's thirty-one-year tenure as a professor of chemistry at San Jose State University. With an eye on his post-retirement career, he spent fifteen years honing his home winemaking skills. Along the way, he worked three summers in the research department at Paul Masson Winery, with the urge to graduate to full-time professional vintner growing stronger as time went on.

"We didn't have much money, so at first we were looking around for an existing winery that might be available," they remember. By chance, Lanny met the owners of Stony Ridge Winery. "We cut a deal where I would become their consulting winemaker and was allowed to craft my own wine under their roof." The Replogles eventually purchased the old George True winery and named it Fenestra, which means window in Latin. In 1976, they were the first small, premium winery to open in Livermore Valley.

Realizing that Rhone-style wines are ideally suited to Livermore Valley's *terroir*, Replogle planted six acres of Syrah, Mourvedre, and Grenache. He locally sources 60 percent of Fenestra's grapes, with the remainder from Lodi. "Our Lodi connection started with an introduction to Ron Silva of Silvaspoons Vineyards. He was growing excellent Portuguese varieties—and I wanted to make Port from his classic varieties." Eventually, the Replogles began turning Fenestra's own Portuguese grapes into table and dessert wines.

Lanny savors choreographing an array of grapes into Fenestra's most popular blend, True Red (named in remembrance of George True). This signature wine is

Fenestra Winery provides a great place to picnic.

Fran and Lanny Replogle with one of their award-winning wines

Photo courtesy of The Independent Magazine

Fall at Fenestra Winery

a complex blend of more than fifteen varieties. "That's the one we make in the greatest quantity, around eighteen hundred cases." The Replogles are proud of their extensive wine list, and Fran says you can usually find them pouring more than twenty wines in the tasting room.

Creators of award-winning wines for more than thirty-five years, the Replogles have earned numerous accolades, including four Gold medals at the Orange County Fair, the coveted Unanimous Gold and Chairman's Award at the Riverside International Wine Competition, and Best Red Wine of Show at the Bay Area Wine Competition.

Lanny turned over the winemaking reins to Brent Amos in 2007. "Of course I still monitor the wine-making process," he says, "but Brent was my assistant for the previous two years and I completely trust him."

Lanny and Brent say they are always on the lookout for new and unusual varieties. "We also both believe in making good wines at a reasonable price, and we are pleased to offer our wines in a friendly, historic setting."

Even if you're a teetotaler, a visit to Fenestra is worth it just to savor the nineteenth-century California ranch setting. Visitors love to picnic creekside in the shade of sprawling trees with timeless vistas of the vine rows.

GarréVineyard and
Winery and Café Garré
7986 Tesla Road
Livermore, CA 94550
(925) 371-8200

Website: www.garrewinery.com
Email: garre@garrewinery.com

- Tasting room: Friday-Sunday, 11:30–5:00

- Established: 1997

- Owners: Robert and Carol Molinaro;
  Winemaker: Wayne Re; Executive Chef: Ty Turner

- Annual production: 2,500 cases

- Varieties: Cabernet Sauvignon, Cabernet Franc, Petite
  Sirah, Syrah, Rosé, Chardonnay, Sauvignon Blanc, Port,
  Bordeaux-style blend, and Merlot

- Wine club: Garré Wine Club

A Glass from the Past, a Toast to the Future

When I first visited Garré Winery, I wondered why there was no one around with the last name of Garré.

Gina Cardera, vice president of operations and daughter of founder Bob Molinaro, solved the mystery. "That's because my father named our winery in honor of our Tuscan roots and to pay homage to my great grandmother, Rosa 'Nonna' Garré."

The art of crafting homemade wine was passed down from the Old Country through the generations to Bob Molinaro. "During prohibition, my dad's family made wine at their 'summer home' in Glen Ellen," says Cardera. "When my dad was a child, the grapes would come by train to San Francisco and all of the uncles would get together and make wine."

As we dined on the Café Garré outdoor patio, Cardera describd their Profound Secret—a field blend of the five Bordeaux varieties—Cabernet Franc, Merlot, Cabernet Sauvignon, Malbec and Petit Verdot which Garré grows on the estate. Once picked,

Tasting Room at Garré Vineyard & Winery

she said, they stay together through the entire winemaking process. "Profound Secret is one of our most enjoyable wines, and it's also one of our newest. It's something we've wanted to do for quite a while."

Garré has recently planted a new estate vineyard of Sangiovese, Primitivo, and Petite Sirah. They source additional Petite Sirah and Sauvignon Blanc from just around the corner, and their Touriga and Tempranillo come from just a few miles away on Mines Road.

The practice of growing twenty acres of their own grapes, with the remainder sourced nearby, Cardera says, allows Garré to control all aspects of the growing cycle, from irrigation and dropping fruit to deciding exactly when to pick.

In addition to offering a vineyard, winery, café, and tasting room, Garré is also home to two impressive event centers. The 6,000-square-foot Garré Grand Pavilion

Photo courtesy of Thomas C. Wilmer

Vineyards at Garré

Weddings and events are hosted at Garré Vineyard & Winery.

Center is across a sprawling lawn from the café, and they also manage the Martinelli Conference and Event Center next door.

The pavilion is a popular wedding venue with an adjacent staging area under a massive oak tree that serves as a favorite area for photo shoots. Garré maintains a strict one-wedding-per-day policy, so guests feel a true sense of ownership. The Martinelli Center is a more traditional conference facility. Offering an extensive array of sophisticated, high-tech equipment, it serves as an ideal venue for corporate meetings. The beautiful Hacienda-style building set amongst the vineyard features an intimate courtyard with an outdoor fireplace, which also makes the Martinelli a popular choice for a destination wedding.

In addition to the wine club, tasting room, and event center sales, the charming Café Garré is a popular place to sip a glass or two, either al fresco on the patio or inside. "Our Executive Chef, Ty Turner, came on board just three months after we opened," Cardera says. In addition to the café, he is also an integral part of all events.

Café Garré offers a Mediterranean-inspired menu. Lunch is served seven days a week, and dinner is offered on Friday nights during the summer in conjunction with the weekly outdoor concert series. A classic Italian-themed dinner is hosted every Wednesday evening and attracts those interested in trying their hand at bocce ball on the adjacent courts. Sometimes customers are intimidated to play, Cardera says. "I tell them, 'Don't worry. If you can hold a glass of wine in one hand and a bocce ball in the other, you have the game pretty much licked!' That sets them at ease, and they go on and play and everyone has a great time."

Summing up all that Garré has to offer, Cardera says, "We provide a gracious environment where guests can experience our Mediterranean-themed restaurant, enjoy elegant weddings, utilize the state of the art meeting space, and savor our hand-crafted small-lot wines." It truly is a fusion of Old-World hospitality and New-World technology.

La Rochelle Winery
5443 Tesla Road
Livermore, CA 94550
(925) 243-6442

Website: www.lrwine.com
Email: pinotnoir@lrwine.com

- Tasting room: daily, noon–4:00; flights available
  wine-only and with cheese pairings

- Established: 2003

- Owner: Steven Kent Mirassou
  Winemaker: Tom Stutz

- Annual production: 3,000 cases

- Varieties: Pinot Noir, Pinot Gris, Pinot Blanc

- Wine club: Pinot Noir Program wine club

A Passion for Pinot

*L*a Rochelle was named in honor of Steven Kent Mirassou's ancestral hometown in France, 106 miles north of Bordeaux. In 1852, Mirassou's great-great-great grandfather, Pierre Pellier, emigrated from La Rochelle to the sleepy Santa Clara Valley. At the time, the valley was reverentially dubbed "the valley of heart's delight"—as virtually anything that was planted came up a winner. Pellier harvested his first grapes in 1854, returned to France, and brought back more than one hundred Old World cuttings, including Pinot Noir and Chardonnay from Burgundy, as well as Bordeaux and Rhone varietals.

Pellier's daughter, Henrietta, married neighboring vintner Pierre Mirassou, who established the Mirassou legacy and thrived through Prohibition by selling grapes for sacramental wine and to home wine makers. In 1961, fourth-generation family members Norbert and Edmund pioneered the rush to establish world-class vineyards in Monterey County. The Mirassou brand continued in the family until 2003, when the Gallo Corporation purchased the brand, rights to the name, and inventory.

Photo courtesy of The Independent Magazine

Winemaker Steven Kent Mirassou tasting Pinot Noir at La Rochelle Winery

Outside the Tasting Room at La Rochelle Winery

Mirassou explains that many people who have been in the wine business for multiple generations don't really know how to do anything else. "Some of my earliest memories are of running around the cellars and working at the family winery. Wine has always been on the family table, in celebrations, and a part of everyday living in my family."

Subsequent to Gallo purchasing the Mirassou brand in 2003, his cousins created La Rochelle as a Monterey County brand specializing in Pinot Noir, Chardonnay, and Merlot, with their winery facility located in San Jose.

In 2005, the rest of the family no longer wanted to remain in the wine business, so Mirassou purchased La Rochelle from his cousins and brought the brand to Livermore.

"There's a lot of great wine made in the world," he says "but wine without passion, without emotion, and without a back-story—it's just a nice-tasting beverage." Mirassou believes emphatically that wine serves as an ideal vehicle for connecting friends and family.

Part of his mission, he says, is to honor his family's past accomplishments. "I have the opportunity to delve into areas my winemaking ancestors were not able to venture. My goal is to accomplish some of the things they were not able to get quite right as winemakers."

Mirassou believes nothing of consequence can be achieved in life unless you are passionate about what you are doing—and this is no roadblock for him or those he works with. La Rochelle specializes in world-class Burgundian varietals sourced from premier California and Oregon vineyards. "We source only from growers who are as passionate about growing world-class fruit as we are about making world-class wine."

La Rochelle treats every clone as a separate wine, making each one in 1.5-ton, open-top fermenters, cold-soaking, using minimal SO_2, with extended maceration and barrel aging (compared to most high-end producers). All the wines are bottled without filtration or fining. The winery produces 95 percent Pinot Noir, with small quantities of Blanc, Gris, and Meunier. Winemaker Tom Stutz, formerly the winemaker at Mirassou since the early 1980s, believes in highlighting the complexity of Pinot Noir (his favorite grape) and allowing as many of the variety's variables as possible to shine through.

French oak is used in large part because it tends to bolster the mid-palate of the wine, providing a sense of roundness and shape. La Rochelle tends to use significantly more French than American oak. "The aromatics of French oak and the structuring effects of French barrels work better with a majority of the Pinot Noir we harvest," Mirassou says.

La Rochelle does not own any vineyards but sources fruit from eighteen vineyards located in eleven appellations (Willamette and Umpqua Valleys of Oregon, Anderson Valley, Russian River Valley, Sonoma Coast, Santa Cruz Mountains, Chalone, Santa Lucia Highlands, Monterey, Arroyo Seco, and Carneros). All but the Oregon fruit is brought to Livermore; La Rochelle's Oregon grapes are processed at the Brandborg Winery in Elkton, Oregon.

Mirassou is truly passionate about sharing his wine and his family's story. "It's what I love doing the most," he says. "In the end, we should all worry less, explore a lot, and drink more good wine!"

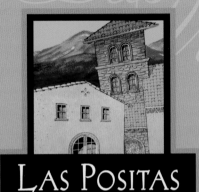

Las Positas Vineyards
682 Pinnacle Place
Livermore, CA 94550
(925) 449-WINE

Website:
www.laspositasvineyards.com
Email:
LPVwines@att.net

- Tasting room: weekends, noon–5

- Established: November 2006

- Owner/winemaker: Lisa Maier

- Annual production: 750 cases

- Varieties: Chardonnay, Cabernet Sauvignon, Petite Sirah, Barbera, Tempranillo, and White Muscat dessert wine (blends available starting in 2013)

- Wine club: Club Rancho Las Positas

Relive the History, Admire the Beauty

The process of translating one's dreams and visions into a tangible reality is sometimes a long road. Minnesota native Lisa Maier moved to Milpitas, California, as a youngster. When Maier—who holds a master's degree in taxation from Golden Gate University—retired as a CPA, she decided to manifest her longtime dream of becoming a winemaker and winery owner. But it was easier said than done.

Las Positas Vineyards remains a work in progress as Maier weaves through the maze of planning and building regulations and permits for her elegant new Spanish/Mediterranean-style winery, which has an anticipated completion date of fall 2011. Her husband, Lothar, offers his assistance with business decisions and dealing with governmental regulations, but by choice, Las Positas Vineyards is Maier's baby.

The couple decided to entirely replant the Kalthoff Commons acreage (the site of the new winery and tasting room), which they purchased in 2006. "Most of the neighboring vineyards were planted in single varietals," Maier says, "but we wanted an array of our own targeted varieties so we could produce 100 percent

Preliminary view of Las Positas Vineyards Tasting Room

estate-grown wines." In the interim, she sources Livermore grapes until her own plantings mature. "Our 2011 harvest will be the first estate-grown crop produced in our facility that will be saleable in 2013." The couple selected Cabernet Sauvignon as Las Positas' signature wine. "Cabernet is a noble variety that has survived the test of time, and it does exceptionally well in Livermore Valley," Maier notes.

*Lisa Maier and son, Karl,
in their Chardonnay vineyard*

She specifically planted varietals such as Petit Verdot and Malbec for blending, but Maier says her ability to produce blends remains limited until the vines mature. "I look forward to the time when we have our own spice rack of varietals to choose from. Experimenting is not only unique in the art of blending but part of the fun of winemaking!"

The new Las Positas facility will have its own bottling line,

Lisa Maier with Las Positas Vineyards wines

and Maier's enthusiasm about it is palpable. "We will be able to control all phases: growing, fermentation, aging, and production, including bottling."

In the meantime, as Maier continues to navigate the bureaucratic gauntlet, she concurrently produces some exceptional, award-winning wines sourced from Livermore Valley grapes. She explains, "We made the decision to purchase grapes from the Livermore Valley and specifically from vineyard owners who share our passion and philosophy of growing the best grapes possible. For example, our 2007 Cabernet Sauvignon and Petite Sirah come from the acclaimed Casa De Vinas Covarrubias Vineyards."

Las Positas Vineyards quickly carved out its niche and established a remarkable reputation for finely crafted, ultra premium boutique wines. Maier's very first release, a 2007 Chardonnay, won silver medals at the Alameda, Orange County, and California state fairs.

As a testimonial to her tenacity and can-do attitude, in the midst of multi-tasking in three different directions, Maier greeted me with a relaxed, radiant smile at the Las Positas Vineyards combination warehouse and tasting room located in a Livermore commercial business park.

The couple explains that when they started the operation, they wanted their winery's name to represent the Livermore Valley. While researching potential candidates, they discovered that Rancho Las Positas was the name of Robert Livermore's ranch, and they were amazed to discover that the name was not already taken. As they say, the rest is history.

Stop by for a visit at Lisa Maier's Las Positas Vineyards tasting room, and discover for yourself the distinctive character of their unique clonal varieties—an experience in which the Chardonnay is just as yummy as the Cabernet Sauvignon.

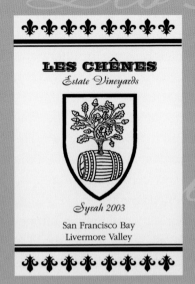

Les Chênes Estate Vineyards

5562 Victoria Lane
Livermore, CA 94550
(925) 373-1662

Website: www.leschenesvine.com
Email: leschenesvine@aol.com

- Tasting room: weekends, noon–4:30 and by appointment; $5 fee (waived with purchase)

- Established: vines planted, 1999; tasting room opened, 2007

- Owners: Candice and Richard Dixon (winemaker)

- Annual production: 1,200 cases

- Varieties: Roussanne, Mourvedre, Viognier, Syrah, Grenache, Deux Rouges, Deux Blancs and Deux Soeurs

- Wine club: Les Amis de Les Chênes Wine Club

Rhone Renaissance in Livermore Valley

The long and narrow French valley of the Rhone is renowned for its sophisticated and complex, yet gentle, blends. There are lots of parallels between the Rhone and Livermore Valleys—so it's no surprise that winemaker Richard Dixon and his wife, Candice, decided to specialize in Rhone varietals.

Experiencing Les Chênes ("the oaks" in French) is about the closest thing to pastoral France that you'll find in Livermore Valley. The setting of Les Chênes, with its intoxicating, timeless vistas of rolling hills and fields of grape vines, will make you feel as if you've stepped into a beautiful oil painting set in the French countryside.

The Dixons are enamored with the subtle style of French Rhone-style wines. "We farm our vineyard with reverence and let the vine tell us what it can do," they say. "We believe in letting the grapes express themselves."

In the 1990s, the Dixons were employed in the packaging sector of the wine and spirits industry and began growing Pinot Noir in Sonoma County. When they moved to Livermore Valley in 1999, the couple purchased their Victoria Lane property. They

Winery owners Richard and Candice Dixon (center) and their family

soon contracted with Wente to plant an array of Rhone-inspired varietals, including Roussanne, Syrah, Mourvedre, and Grenache Noir.

Les Chênes is smaller than a boutique winery, producing about 1,200 cases annually. "We do most everything here, as we have our own crusher, de-stemmer, presses, and tanks," the Dixons explain. Their production is primarily estate grown, but for a few of their blends they use locally sourced Cabernet Sauvignon, Viognier, Chardonnay, and, occasionally, Zinfandel.

Explaining their winemaking philosophy, the Dixons say, "The very first and most important thing is to do it right. Secondly, we try to make wines that are more reflective of French style, European style, and Rhone style in preference over New World wines."

The tasting room, designed and built by the Dixons, is where Candice showcases her love of food and wine pairings. "The French do not drink without eating, and

Winemaker Richard Dixon

Richard and Candice Dixon, owners of Les Chênes Estate Vineyards

View from Les Chênes Estate Vineyards

they do not eat without drinking—so we follow that same style with our cheeses and various pairings."

"We vacation vicariously through our friends," Candice says, "since our job here is truly 24-7. Right now we're running a contest called Take Les Chênes Around the World. When our customers travel they take pictures of our bottles from all corners of the world and send them back to us."

But there are paybacks for maintaining a peerless passion and non-stop attention to detail: The Dixons opened the tasting room in April 2007 and just three months later were named Best New Winery in the East Bay by *Diablo* magazine.

The Dixons say they didn't want Les Chênes to be another in a long list of Livermore Valley wineries that specialize in Cab, Chardonnay, and Merlot. "We wanted to distinguish ourselves by following our passion for Rhone-style wines." They did extensive research on climates and soils and discovered that Rhone varietals thrive in this valley. "It's worked out extremely well for us."

There are two signature wines at Les Chênes: Deux Rouges and Deux Blancs ("Two Red" and "Two White"). Shortly after opening, the Dixons received a high honor: the French Counsel General in San Francisco requested a visit to their estate. His favorite cuvee turned out to be their Chardonnay Viognier blend. "That's how Deux Blancs earned its moniker—and it has turned out to be by far our most popular white wine!" Candice says proudly.

Gargouille ("Gargoyle" in French) is another popular Les Chênes blend. It's an estate Mourvedre with Syrah and just a bit of a red-currant-flavored Zinfandel.

The Dixons say their goal is to follow a European model. Their wines have structure and balance. They're not overwhelmingly fruity, and most importantly, they're very food friendly. "We create a healthy, balanced environment so that nature expresses her voice," they say. "Our job is to listen."

Little Valley Winery
739 Main Street
Pleasanton, CA 94566
(925) 862-9006

Website:
littlevalleywinery-lavender.com
Email: javafixx@tdl.com

- Tasting room: Thursday–Saturday, noon–6pm; Sunday, noon–5pm

- Established: 2000

- Owners: Sandi Bohner and Bill Webster (winemaker)

- Annual production: 2,300 cases

- Varieties: Livermore-grown Cabernet Sauvignon, Tempranillo, Chardonnay, Sauvignon Blanc, Cabernet Franc, Pure Decadence Port, California Champagne, California Raspberry Champagne, California Almond Champagne, Rabbit's Blush, White Zinfandel, Livermore Petite Sirah, Zinfandel, Gypsy Blend, 5150 Red Table Wine, Ambrosia, and Albarino

- Wine club: Rabbit's Tale Wine Club

Follow the White Rabbit to Your Pleasanton Downtown Destination

*A*n innocent bike ride down Tesla Road changed the lives of Sandi Bohner and her husband, Bill, when they stopped in for a visit to Garré Winery. The couple chatted with the owners, and before they knew it, Sandi was the pastry chef and special events coordinator at the new Café Garré, and Bill was involved with Garré's winemaking and special events.

The couple's wine industry experience had been limited to hosting winemaker dinners at their Pleasanton Decadent Dessert Café—one of five such establishments that Sandi has owned (some in partnership with her husband) since 1983. Through their exposure to the Livermore Valley wine industry at Garré and Sandi's work at various local wineries, the couple became a part of the local vintners' community and were often encouraged to start their own winery. In 2000 they made the leap and launched Little Valley Winery, planting a two-acre vineyard on their Sunol property.

Sandi Bohner and Bill Webster of Little Valley Winery

Photo courtesy of The Independent Magazine

In 2001, they unveiled their tasting room in quaint, downtown Sunol. Utilizing Sandi's extensive background as a food service professional and pastry chef, the couple offered a café and espresso bar in their tasting room, which also became a popular local music venue. Before long, *Diablo* magazine proclaimed the Little Valley Winery gathering spot as the number one place to hang out, eat, drink wine, and listen to music in the entire San Francisco East Bay area.

In 2009, when they opened the doors of their new tasting room and retail facility in downtown Pleasanton, it was the first tasting room to

Outside Little Valley Winery in downtown Pleasanton

grace the area in more than several decades. "It was a great move for us, as the city hosts so many fairs, parades, and festivals," Bill says. The Little Valley Winery tasting room is replete with one of the region's largest selections of wine related gift items.

Sandi also specializes in lavender-based products. Presently, the couple offers more than sixty products for sale online, and Sandi teaches lavender cooking classes.

In 2000, Bill and Sandi were among the first in the region to realize that the Iberian varietal Tempranillo was ideally suited to the region's *terroir*, and it became their flagship wine. "This noble, world-class Spanish varietal is a lighter red wine with an excellent, strong, tannic structure," Bill explains. "Because of this, it is ready to drink in as early as two years, but like a Portuguese Port, it can lay down for ten or more. The primary component of a traditional Port is Tempranillo." Their first Tempranillo won a gold medal at the California State Fair. "And it makes a delicious sangria!" Sandi adds.

As a winemaker, Bill explains that he has the same philosophy he honed early in his hi-tech, military, aerospace career. "I have chosen to make products that people really need and truly benefit from using. Today, my philosophy remains the same—to make something that people really enjoy, and that's fine artisan wines!"

In addition to their flagship Tempranillo, Little Valley's offerings include other Iberian wines, as well as locally grown Petite Sirah, Sauvignon Blanc, and Cabernet Sauvignon. Beyond Livermore Valley appellation wines, their Tempranillo is sourced from Tracy Hills.

Bill's winemaking strategy is to source the best California grapes, and Little Valley is a proud Livermore Valley Winery with an offering of great local and Iberian wines.

Longevity Wines
35 Rickenbacker Circle
Livermore, CA 94550
(925) 551-6373/
(888) 325-WINE

Website:
www.longevitywines.com
Email:
plong@longevitywines.com

- Tasting room: Weekends, noon–5, and by appointment; $5 tasting fee for groups of eight or more (waived with purchase or keep the glass)

- Established: July 2008

- Owners: Phil (winemaker) and Debra Long

- Annual production: 1,000 cases

- Varieties: Chenin Blanc, Viognier, Chardonnay, Syrah Rosé, Barbera, Merlot, Syrah, Cabernet Sauvignon, Petite Sirah, Rhone-style blend, Mourvedre, Bordeaux-style blend, Sangiovese, Zinfandel, and a Zinfandel Port

- Wine club: Longevity Wine Club

Longevity—Not Just a Wine, but a Lifestyle

Like so many boutique winery owners, Phil Long has a day job as creative director for a large design/marketing firm, while his wife, Debra, works as the office manager for the Danville Area Chamber of Commerce. But they have another full-time job, too.

In 2008, the Longs opened their urban-style winery situated a couple of blocks from the Livermore Airport, but their dream was nurtured through a decade-long passion for weekend wine-tasting adventures.

They remember the moment they became fascinated by wine: when they first savored the essence of fruit while sipping a glass of BV Syrah. "From then on it was a rush downhill," they say.

The couple's never-ending fascination with wine tasting led to their creation of the Longevity Wine Club, a very successful web-based group. The Longs visited wineries in pursuit of exceptional offerings for their wine club, featuring a different appellation each month. Over the years, they spoke with hundreds of winemakers from across California. "We learned as much as we could from each winemaker and took meticulous notes. It's amazing how fast

Longevity Winery at Holiday time

your palette develops when you are tasting wine all the time."

The Longs spent years sourcing the best wines from every appellation they could find. The natural progression, as it is for most who are bitten by the wine bug, led them to commence crafting their own wines in a garage.

When they relocated to Northern California, the Longs shifted from a garage operation to crafting the "Longevity" wines (a play on their last name) at their mentors' Livermore Valley custom crush facilities.

Although their current annual production hovers around 1,000 cases, they have a five-year plan to reach 2,500. But while the Longs have plans for growth, Phil says, "We enjoy the challenge of making a wide variety of wines, and we strive to find grapes that are high in quality, rather than large quantities."

For the Longs, the wine industry is as much a way of life as it is a business. "We are in it because we love it," they say.

Winemaker Phil Long

Phil and Debra Long with winery dog, PressTon

The couple currently purchases all of their fruit, but their goal is to own a vineyard in the near future. "Presently, we are concentrating on getting our brand-name recognition out there."

They are firm believers in the exceptional grapes grown in the Livermore AVA, but they also source grapes from Contra Costa, Lodi, the Sierra foothills, the San Francisco Bay appellation, and elsewhere. In addition to single varietals, including an exceptional Chardonnay, they craft two blends: Longevity Rhone and BDX Longevity Bordeaux-style blend. "Those are the ones we do best," they say, mentioning that they barrel age Longevity reds for twenty-four to thirty-six months, with a minimum of a few months in the bottle before release.

Just before I left their winery, Phil Long reflected on his lengthy journey from Cal Poly to Livermore. Trained as an architect, he finds that he uses the same skills he honed in school: sophisticated artistic discernment, creative design acumen, and brand marketing savvy. From designing the labels to building the tasting room themselves to sensitively crafting the wine, Long's training as an architect dovetails in surprising ways with his career as a winemaker.

Summing up the Longevity winemaking philosophy, Phil said with a smile, "Winemaking can be defined in about four basic steps: harvest, crush, press, and age. But it's in the next one hundred steps that you learn to make a truly good wine, and the next thousand steps define who you are as a winemaker." The Longs believe it isn't as much about the wine as it is the entire experience. "Yes, my job is to put great wine on the table, but I hope that people go away remembering the entire social experience, the enjoyable conversations and interactions."

Visit Longevity's urban tasting room and you will see this philosophy in action. Prepare to be graciously welcomed by two smiling characters who greet each and every visitor with warmth and cheer. You'll feel like you've just arrived at a good friend's cocktail party.

McGrail Vineyards
and Winery
5600 Greenville Road
Livermore, CA 94550
(925) 215-0717

Website:
mcgrailvineyards.com
Email:
heather@mcgrailvineyards.com
Facebook and Twitter

- Tasting room: Friday–Monday, noon–4:30, and by appointment; $5 tasting fee (waived with purchase)
- Established: 1999 (tasting room and winery opened 2008)
- Owner/winemakers: Jim, Ginger, and Heather McGrail, and local consulting winemakers
- Annual production: 2,500 cases
- Varieties: Cabernet Sauvignon, Chardonnay, Petite Syrah
- Wine club: Holy McGrail Wine Club

It's a Family Affair

*W*hen it comes right down to it, the McGrail Vineyard experience is as much about family and friends as it is about wines and vines.

In fact, throughout the Livermore Valley you will regularly meet husbands and wives, and often their children and grandchildren, too, who are all intimately involved in the wine industry. This familial dynamic is a very endearing motif—and it's especially radiant at McGrail. I was just as impressed with the friendly, jovial, and tender interactions between father and mother, Jim and Ginger, and daughter, Heather, as I was with their fine wines.

McGrail Vineyards and Winery is perched on a Crane Ridge bluff-top with panoramic vistas. The entry reveals a stately tasting room backed by undulating fields of grape and fronted by a sprawling lawn that beckons as a festive party venue, complete with bocce-ball courts. And then there's Jim McGrail's iconic, eye-catching 1946 Mac truck parked out by the entry gate.

When the McGrails purchased their property on Greenville Road, it was set up as a horse ranch. But soon, family friends Phil and Julie Wente would counsel the McGrails to plant sixteen acres of Cabernet Sauvignon vines. The results were so exceptional that

McGrail Vineyards & Winery

the Steven Kent Winery annually purchased their entire harvest.

Eventually, the dynamics of sourcing grapes shifted, and the McGrails decided to open their own winery. Good thing they did—there's nothing more gratifying than receiving full credit for growing and producing some of California's finest Cabernet Sauvignon.

McGrail also crafts Cabernet blends in conjunction with a barrel program that provides a variety of price points. According to Heather, "Our James Vincent is 100 percent French oak, while our Reserve is 70 percent new oak (barrel aged for three years, with four months in the bottle before release), and our regular offering is all neutral oak, with a smoothness that makes it easier to drink for the beginning Cab lover."

They use a combination of French, Hungarian, and American oak to achieve maximum complexity. McGrail wines typically exhibit

*Estate Vineyards at
McGrail Vineyards & Winery*

Jim, Ginger, and Heather McGrail

Inside McGrail Vineyards & Winery

dark cherry, chocolate, and caramel flavors, and their neutral oak wine has a fruity taste. "It's a very sippable wine that entry-level Cab lovers really enjoy," Heather says.

She points to her mom and winemaker, Ginger, with pride and a warm smile. "She has the best nose of all of us. My dad has the love and passion for great Cabernet, but it's my mom who has the keenest taste and scent for outstanding wine."

The level of alcohol in McGrail wines tends to run between 14 and 15 percent, and when I asked Jim about this, he winked and said proudly, "Heck, we're Irish!" McGrail wines bring out complex aromatic tastes and a balanced fruit forward expression. Thus, without reading the label, one might not realize that the wines are typically on the higher end of the scale.

All of McGrail's Cabernet is estate grown, but they have recently added an outstanding Chardonnay, sourced from nearby Wente and Wisner family farms. The McGrails are just now adding Petite Sirah to their tightly focused portfolio. "All of our grapes are sourced locally in the Livermore Valley," Heather says. "As long as we can get the fruit, we always want to use only locally grown grapes."

Jim McGrail notes that to achieve optimum fruit characteristics they drop an incredible amount of berries to net the targeted three and a half tons per acre. By thinning the clusters, the remaining fruit receives maximum benefit of the vine's nutrients and energy. McGrail adds, "It makes you cry to walk through the fields and see all the dropped fruit, but it's all about quality, not quantity."

Heather, who handles sales and marketing, summed up the philosophy at McGrail Vineyards and Winery; "Without a doubt, our vineyard is the most important aspect of the winery. With a firm foundation as growers, we intimately understand that to get great juice you must start with great fruit." She concluded, "Our goal in the winery is to ensure that we nurture the product and not ruin what Mother Nature gave us." And, of course, they plan on continuing to produce the best and most drinkable Cabernet from the Livermore Valley.

Mitchell Katz Winery
1188 Vineyard Avenue
Pleasanton, CA 94566
(925) 931-0744

Website:
mitchellkatzwinery.com
Email:
mitchellkatzwine@aol.com

- Tasting room: Thursday–Sunday, noon–5 (group tastings by appointment)
- Established: 1998
- Owners: Alicia and Mitchell Katz (winemaker)
- Annual production: 8,500 cases
- Varieties: Chardonnay, Pinot Blanc, Pinot Grigio, Petite Sirah, Cabernet Sauvignon, Sangiovese, Merlot, Syrah, Wesley's Blend, Zinfandel, and various Ports
- Wine club: Brick Clique Wine Club

A Little History in Every Bottle

*A*s I rolled down the palm fringed lane to Mitchell Katz winery, I was mesmerized by the stately, two-story, red-brick edifice that towered above. It was like a fortress, complete with plank cellar doors, shuttered dormers, and ridge-top cupola.

This elegant beacon of Livermore Valley was erected in 1887 and opened its doors as John Crellin's Ruby Hill Winery. Sadly, following years of abandonment and a fire in 1989, the bricks all came tumbling down. Fortunately the vintage bricks were saved, reassembled, and mortared back in place. Today, the painstakingly reconstructed building serves as the home of Mitchell Katz winery.

As a child, Katz would spend the summers with his grandparents in England, assisting his grandfather as he concocted variations on the theme of winemaking with watermelons, strawberries, and other high-fructose candidates in his garage.

Entrance to Mitchell Katz Winery

A union steamfitter by trade, Katz began crafting his own "medicinal" wine at home in the late 1980s. By the early 1990s, Katz was propelled to the next level when his wife, Alicia, introduced him to Phil Wente of Wente Vineyards, who gave Katz entrée to pick the grapes left on the vines after the mechanical harvesters finished their work. When Katz opened his winery in 1998, it was the sixteenth post-Prohibition winery in Livermore Valley.

Katz still savors the buzz and hum of the winemaking experience. "You have so much to do in such a short period of time. It is also the joy of sharing a piece of yourself—going to a dinner party and bringing a bottle of wine—something that you made with your own hands—watching it go from the dirt to the dinner table!"

Katz loves producing fruit-forward—not watered down—wine. His fruit is macerated from ten to twenty-one days on the skins, creating big, full-bodied wines with strong tannins. He produces primarily

Entrance into Mitchell Katz Winery

Winemaker Mitch Katz

Night view of Mitchell Katz Winery

single-vineyard wines and works closely in the fields with roughly eight Livermore Valley growers.

The close working relationship with his growers creates a win-win partnership. "I put their vineyard designation on my bottles, and they become a proud part of the entire process," he says. "If you just throw their Sangiovese in a tank with a bunch of other grapes, no one knows which part made it good and which part made it bad. I couldn't do this without them. My grandfather always said that you can't make good wine from bad grapes . . . but you can sure make bad wine from good grapes. And, I've never been one who believes that a great wine has to be expensive."

A firm advocate of Livermore Valley viticulture, Katz says, "I think Petite Sirah is the varietal that is most representative of our AVA, and it was Jim Concannon, right here in Livermore, who was the first to put it on the wine map."

Because of Livermore Valley's diverse environmental influences, Katz can create two completely different wines from the same grape variety. "For example, we source our estate Petite Sirah here on the west side, but I have another Petite Sirah from Falling Star Vineyards located on the far eastside. It's a completely different wine, much softer and more approachable."

Katz's west side estate wine is bigger in tannins and better for laying down and aging—although they have both won numerous awards. The estate Petite Sirah placed in the Top 100 Wines in the San Francisco Chronicle a few years ago and has won two gold medals since. The 2006 Falling Star first-release Petite Sirah won Best of Show at the Orange County Fair among a selection of 3,000 wines.

At Mitchell Katz Winery, you can enjoy handcrafted, vineyard-designated wines that showcase the microclimates and soil variations of the historic Livermore Valley.

Murrieta's Well Winery
3005 Mines Road
Livermore, CA 94550
(925) 456-2395

Website:
www.murrietaswell.com
Email:
tastingroom@murrietaswell.com

- Tasting room: May-October: Daily 11-4:30; November-April: Wednesday-Sunday, 11-4:30; $10 tasting fee

- Established: 1990

- Owners: Wente Family; Winemaking Team: Karl D. Wente, Winemaker; Sergio Traverso; Consulting Winemaker

- Annual production: 5,000–8,000 cases

- Varieties: Cabernet Sauvignon, Merlot, Cabernet Franc, Petit Verdot, Touriga Francesca, Tempranillo, Zinfandel, Souzao, Touriga Nacional, Sauvignon Blanc, and Semillon

- Amenities: weddings, receptions, and events in the Barrel Room, located in the historic, century-old winery building with capacity for up to 120 people

- Wine club: Silver Spur Wine Club

Unforgettable Estate Blends from California's Livermore Valley

*I*t's fitting that Murrieta's Well is set off by itself down a winding road away from the Tesla Road wine trail. Back in the Gold Rush era, one of California's most legendary banditos, Joaquin Murrieta (dubbed the "Robin Hood of El Dorado"), would sometimes frequent this tranquil spot. Murrieta was known to water his steeds at an artesian well on the property while en route to sell his booty in Mexico.

There's another intriguing layer to the historic property's tale—Louis Mel, a French immigrant and successful entrepreneur, visited the property and realized the site's gravelly soil was remarkably similar to the *terroir* of Bordeaux's premier vineyards. Mel says in an interview from the 1930s, "I was enchanted with the place. Its soil and climate seemed much like the countryside of La Belle France, where we had both spent our younger days. So I took Mrs. Mel to see it and she agreed it was a lovely spot. In 1884 we bought the place and made it our home, and as the Wentes and Concannons and other neighbors around us had vineyards, I decided to plant vines, too."

Photo courtesy of The Independent Magazine

Sergio Traverso, co-founder of Murrieta's Well, tends to the estate.

Mel used the hillside location and Murrieta's legendary well to his advantage when he built an ingenious gravity-flow winery. And the story gets better—Mel's wife was close friends with the Marquis de Lur-Saluces, owner of the legendary Château d'Yquem in Bordeaux. With a letter of introduction from his Livermore friend, Charles Wetmore traveled to Bordeaux in 1882 and returned with prized cuttings of Sauvignon Blanc and Semillon from the Château. Both Wetmore and Mel planted the vines that produced the Livermore Sauternes, which for Wetmore won America's first gold medals at the 1889 Paris Exposition.

In the 1930s, Ernest Wente purchased the property and winery from Mel, and the business weathered through the Prohibition era by producing sacramental wine for the Catholic Church.

The Wentes maintained the vineyards until 1990, when Ernest's son, Phil, formed a partnership with Concannons winemaker, Sergio Traverso. They created Murrieta's Well Winery, specializing in Bordeaux, Portuguese, and Spanish varietals. Phil Wente explains that his grandfather, Ernest, "was very familiar with the winery under Mel's tenure before Prohibition and believed strongly in traditional winemaking methods. He would take me around and show me the benefits of a traditional gravity-flow winery. When we started the winery, we carefully restored the building to keep intact its nineteenth-century, hand-wrought character."

According to Karl Wente, Traverso and his uncle Phil created old-world style field blends from the unique combination of original plantings that thrived on the estate. Carolyn Wente adds, "Phil and Sergio decided to continue Mel's legacy by growing and producing the classic Bordeaux blends—Cabernet Sauvignon, Malbec, Merlot, and Cabernet Franc—as well as the white varieties, Sauvignon Blanc and Semillon."

Today at Murrieta's Well, Phil Wente says, "we focus on creating wines that are intrinsically unique in character. We blend small lots of truly distinctive varietals."

Traverso eventually sold his interest in the winery but remains intimately involved as consulting winemaker. As one of Livermore Valley's most revered winemakers, he has a stellar background in viticulture. After graduating from the University of Chile in Santiago, Traverso earned masters and PhD degrees from UC Davis. He went to work in Mexico as technical director for one of North America's oldest wineries before becoming Domaine Chandon's first winemaker. Traverso later worked as a consultant for an array of Napa and Sonoma premier wineries, including Clos du Val, Mondavi, Sterling, Inglenook, and Sonoma-Cutrer. In 1982 he became winemaker at Concannon, when owner Augustin Hunneaus brought him to Livermore Valley. He left Concannon vineyards in 1990 after becoming president and a limited partner there. When Traverso came on board at Murrieta's Well, he says, "Together, with Phil, we resurrected an exquisite wine estate and dedicated ourselves to making wines of character and distinction." Today, he works closely with Karl Wente on a range of unique blended wines.

A fifth-generation Wente, Karl just happens to live in Louis Mel's Victorian-era home adjacent to the historic winery. He says that it was incredibly fun to be a part of the operation and watch his uncle Phil and Sergio Traverso work together. He notes, "They both have such amazing palates, and I have learned so much by working and blending with them. Our vision is very much in the Chateau concept, where everything is grown on the winery's ninety-two acres. Our blends might change from year to year, but we stick to the core Bordeaux cultivars."

A visit to Murrieta's Well is bound to evoke enchanting images of California's past as you stroll around the grounds or do a little tasting in Louis Mel's century-old, brick-and-stone barrel aging room. It's definitely worth the time to come savor the sights and scents of this timeless setting, and taste some excellent Bordeaux-style blends.

Nottingham Cellars &
Satyrs' Pond Winery
2245C South Vasco Road
Livermore, CA 94550
(925) 294-8647

Website:
www.nottinghamcellars.com
Email:
info@nottinghamcellars.com

- Tasting room: Friday–Sunday, noon–4:30, and by appointment; $5 tasting fee (waived with purchase)
- Established: 2009
- Owners: Jeff and Collin (manager/winemaker) Cranor
- Annual production: 1,800 cases
- Varieties: Viognier, Chardonnay, Cabernet Sauvignon, Syrah, Zinfandel, and Pinot Noir. Blends: Meritage and Raphi's Red Blend.
- Wine clubs: Nottingham Cellars and Satyrs' Pond

Fine Living Requires Fine Wine

Long before the advent of Livermore Valley's Nottingham Cellars, Jeff Cranor (partner in a manufacturing company) and his attorney partner created Satyrs' Pond Wine Club based in Burlingame. It started as a fun hobby, Cranor says, to package premium wines, sourced from around California, and sell them at tremendous discounts in relatively large volume to club members.

As the business blossomed, Cranor's son, Collin, started working with his father to handle the shipping and receiving. He then took on responsibility for outside sales. The more involved he became with his father's business, the more intrigued he was with the entire wine industry. Collin began studying the nuances of winemaking, how to source grapes, and barrel maintenance.

"Unfortunately," his father remembers, "as our hobby grew, it started to demand way too much of our time to leave any room for fun—it had grown far beyond a hobby." The two decided that the most viable option was to relocate the Satyrs' Pond operation from Burlingame to Livermore Valley and piggyback the wine club with a traditional winery. Thus was born Nottingham Cellars, with Collin taking the lead as winemaker.

Jeff and Collin Cranor of Nottingham Cellars

What attracted them to the area, Collin says, was Livermore Valley's "incredible history as one of California's earliest producers of award-winning wines, and especially the great wines being produced here today—plus we really felt a connection with the area." The local growers are an essential reason the Cranors decided to solely source Livermore Valley grapes for their Nottingham wines. "They tailor their vineyards to winemakers like us," Collin says. "They're reducing the fruit, reducing the net tonnage per acre, and the quality correspondingly skyrockets. This is an essential reason why you're seeing better and better wines out of Livermore Valley." This is perfect for them, he says, since their mission is to offer the very finest, small-lot Livermore Valley wines.

Collin is impressed with Livermore' Valleys stellar Petite Sirah, Viognier, and Cabernets. He adds that local wineries such as McGrail Vineyards are producing "some awesome Cabs."

Fine Living Requires Fine Wine

As a winemaker, Collin says the old song that great wine is made in the vineyard is true, but he adds that "there are certain things you can do with those grapes in the winemaking process that can make a big difference in the end product." To assist with his winemaking decisions, Collin receives frequent technical input and direction from a veteran Livermore Valley vintner who acts as his behind-the-scenes mentor. "Winemaking is a never-ending learning experience. Every vintage is different, every blend is an experiment, and you just put out the best stuff you have." He uses their signature wine, Raphi's Red Blend, as an example. Getting it "absolutely perfect," he says, took more than one hundred trials.

Nottingham sources French and American oak barrels from a variety of coopers, and they believe that every barrel introduces distinctive characteristics. They've been concentrating on producing Cabernet, Syrah, Petite Sirah, and Malbec, and by processing the same grapes in different barrels, they wind up with divergent characteristics. "And that diversity is ideal for blending," they say.

Their target time for barrel aging ranges from twelve to twenty-four months, and bottle aging is targeted at three to six months. "But as is often the case with a young winery, the consumer is so excited to try the wines that the winemaker is sometimes pressured into releasing the first vintages a few months early," Collin says.

The Cranors are effusive in their praise for Livermore Valley's community spirit. "Everyone out here was such a big help as we were getting established," they say. "It's like a small family—everybody knows everybody and everybody wants to help everybody, because the ultimate goal here is to pump up the valley's reputation and put us on the map as a world-class wine destination."

The mission of this father-and-son team is to offer small-lot, premium Livermore Valley wines at an exceptional value. Check out their urban cellar-tasting room situated on the edge of town and the valley's legendary grape fields. The Cranor family promises that whether you're a newcomer to wine or a connoisseur, they'll provide you with a memorable wine experience.

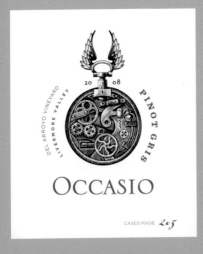

Occasio Winery
2245-B South Vasco Road
Livermore, CA 94550
(925) 371-1987

Website:
www.occasiowinery.com
Email:
info@occasiowinery.com

- Tasting room: Friday–Sunday, noon–5; and by appointment; $5 tasting fee (waived with purchase)

- Established: 2008

- Owner/Winemaker: John Kinney

- Annual production: 1,500 cases

- Varieties: Sauvignon Blanc, Pinot Gris, Merlot, Petite Sirah, Zinfandel, Cabernet Sauvignon, Cabernet Franc, and Petit Verdot

- Wine club: The Occasio Society

True to the Vineyard

Not far from Twin Falls, Idaho, John Kinney grew up in a fifth-generation family of bean farmers. The goal of Idaho growers—whether growing beans or spuds—was to strive for uniformity. But in his world, "a bean was a bean was a bean." So you can imagine Kinney's surprise when cousins from Napa Valley showed up with an armload of finely crafted wines. "That was the very first time anyone brought wine that wasn't in a jug!" he remembers.

The cousins' arrival was an epiphany for the young Kinney, who was fascinated by the diversity of wines. "I was amazed by the artistry and craftsmanship that goes into converting a grape into something that can take such remarkably different directions."

While doing his graduate engineering studies at UC Davis, he says, "the old wine school was not far from my department, and that's when my curiosity about wine started to evolve." Kinney subsequently went to work at the Livermore National Laboratory in the Chemistry and Materials Science Department in 1974. As he'd commute down Tesla Road he'd pass the Wente and Concannon grape fields, but he didn't think too much about the wine industry

Winemaker John Kinney observing one of his vintages

Photo courtesy of *The Independent Magazine*

until Bob Taylor, Kinney's co-worker and friend at the lab, told him about the new winery he was starting. "When I went to visit Bob's winery, I remember distinctly that it was the first time I had ever tasted wine from a barrel. Bob explained how the wine was going to develop over time in the barrel and eventually become a finished product. That's when I realized I didn't know anything about how to predict anything about wine."

Kinney explained that the experience of home wine-making was so gratifying that he made the decision in 2007 to become a professional winemaker. "We applied to become a bonded winery and received our license in August 2008, with our first big harvest that fall," he remembers.

All of Occasio's fruit is locally sourced, as Kinney is a staunch believer in the valley's superior grapes and long history of producing award-winning wines. He's especially enamored with Livermore's Sauvignon Blanc, and in his first year he intro-

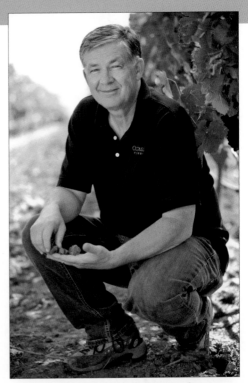

John Kinney in the vineyards

The Tasting Room at Occasio Winery

duced a Loire-style, 100 percent Sauvignon Blanc aged in stainless steel tanks. "In our second year we introduced a barrel fermented Sauvignon Blanc which provides for an interesting comparison." An ardent believer in *sur lie* aging, he uses state-of-the-art, oval-shaped, stainless-steel fermenters. "They're the only ones in the state of California, and the oval shape provides us with a very shallow lees bed that allows for maximum efficiency when we stir the lees."

He also makes a fuller style Pinot Gris and does all of his white wines in stainless steel. For Petite Sirah and Zinfandel, he says, "I think they deserve American oak, and the old admonition that American oak is too fruity is passé. The new, three-year-plus seasoned American oak provides wonderful aging potential. I really like some of the spiciness, and I get more vanilla on the palate."

Kinney is impressed with Livermore Valley's history of producing award-winning Petite Sirah and produces his own exceptional offering. "We are very careful with the extraction of seed tannins on the Petite Sirah," he says. "We have a tendency to press the wine off the skins and seeds before the end of primary fermentation, so we get less alcohol extraction of the tannins." He also crafts a zesty Zinfandel and says it is particularly well-suited for aging in American oak barrels.

When discussing bottle aging his wines before release, he explains there are lots of variables, and like many wineries, "if we run out of a certain vintage, we are sometimes forced to release a wine before reaching its optimum. The wonderful thing is that every day after release, the wine just gets better and better!"

His job as a winemaker, he says, is to translate the essence of the vineyard without altering its identity. "I believe in a minimalist approach to winemaking, where the winemaker's style is best noticed by its absence. Occasio Winery crafts award-winning wines that optimally express the soul of Livermore Valley."

Page Mill Winery

2005
Cabernet Sauvignon
Livermore Valley

VINTED AND BOTTLED BY PAGE MILL WINERY
LIVERMORE, CALIFORNIA
ALCOHOL 14.3% BY VOLUME
CONTAINS SULFITES

Page Mill Winery
1960 S. Livermore Avenue
Livermore, CA 94550
(925) 456-7676

Website:
www.pagemillwinery.com
Email:
info@pagemillwinery.com

- Tasting room: Friday–Sunday, noon–4:30, and by appointment; $5 tasting fee (waived with purchase)
- Established: 1976
- Owners: Dane (winemaker) and Angela Stark
- Annual production: 3,000 cases
- Varieties: Estate organic Petite Sirah, Sauvignon Blanc, Chardonnay, Zinfandel, Cabernet Sauvignon, Cabernet Franc, Pinot Noir; Cabernet and Merlot blends

A Passion for Winemaking

*D*ane Stark's father, Dick, discovered the wine lifestyle while traveling through Europe selling lasers in the early 1970s. According to the younger Stark, that's when his father became so smitten by the wine culture that he "up and quit his job in 1975, dug a hole for a cellar under and adjacent to our Los Altos Hills home on Page Mill Road, and opened Page Mill Winery." Stark was a kid at the time and recalls his excitement. "I thought dad was digging an extension to our swimming pool!"

He went off to college "much preferring beer," but Stark's life transformed when he spent his junior year in Bordeaux, France, studying enology and learning French. "That's when I absolutely fell in love with wine and the winemaking process," he remembers.

During his senior year, Stark took a semester off to work at the winery. It was then that he realized his passion for winemaking, and he joined his father as a full-time employee at Page Mill Winery after graduating in 1989. When his father retired in 1996, Stark took over. In the early years

Winemaker Dane Stark and winery cat

Photo courtesy of The Independent Magazine

Tasting Room at Page Mill Winery

of the business, his father had discovered that he did not enjoy growing grapes and eventually purchased all of them, sourced from appellations across the state, with microclimates to suit the varietals.

Stark continued with his father's model until space limitations at the Page Mill Road facility spurred the family to search for a new property. They considered Healdsburg, Paso Robles, the Santa Cruz Mountains, the Sierra Foothills, and elsewhere. In 2004, they chose the Livermore Valley.

"It was the perfect combination of proximity to our existing South Bay Area clientele and an exceptional growing region," Stark says. But what the Starks and other valley residents appreciate the most, he says, is the support of the local community that values the wine industry for holding back the tide of urban development and preserving the rural lifestyle.

It wasn't long before Stark shifted from his father's model of sourcing grapes from across the state to securing more than 90 percent of his harvest from the Livermore Valley. Now, the only non-local grapes at Page Mill Winery come from the nearby Santa Cruz Mountains.

Stark's favorite Livermore Valley varietal is Petite Sirah (and he points out that Petite Sirah was first introduced to America as a varietal label by Livermore Valley's Concannon Vineyard). He's also a fan of the local Sauvignon Blanc and Cabernet Sauvignon.

He explains the wide diversity of microclimates within the valley and says that, in addition to the area's ideal *terroir*, the coastal maritime weather provides warm, breezy days and cool nights.

Stark's European winemaking style is a product of his early viticultural training in Bordeaux. "I favor under-oaked wines as opposed to over-oaked and medium to medium-soft tannins. It's actually hard to utilize California grapes," he says, "and not wind up with fruit-forward wine."

What Stark is looking for is the perfect balance. "I have been accused of harvesting under-ripe grapes for a long time," he says, but he believes the industry at large is coming around to his method. Stark describes intensely fruit-forward wines as not food friendly, and he believes they do not age as well.

He is exceptionally proud of his Page Mill Dry Rosé, which he has been making for more than a decade, even though, "Rosé was perceived for quite some time as a vino non grata." But fortunately, he explains, "people started making it the right way—dry." It can be serious, elegant, and exceptionally delicious when made without residual sugars, he says. "Those in the south of France always knew this, but we are just realizing it."

Stark works hard to utilize local resources, maximizing sustainable and organic practices whenever possible. But he is careful to avoid the hype that often accompanies these kinds of efforts.

As Stark bid me farewell and walked back to his bottling line, he reminded me, "We like to say, 'Peace through wine—one glass at a time!'" With a twinkle in his eye, he added, " Who knows, if I wasn't making wine, heck, I might be a Zen Buddhist or something like that. But thankfully I am making wine—which is a much easier lifestyle!"

RETZLAFF

CABERNET
SAUVIGNON 60%
MERLOT 40%

LIVERMORE VALLEY
CALIFORNIA

ESTATE BOTTLED

VINTAGE 2004
AGED IN OAK 2 yrs.
OF CASES 634

ALCOHOL 13% BY VOLUME

R.W. Taylor, Winemaker

GROWN, PRODUCED, AND BOTTLED BY
RETZLAFF VINEYARDS
1356 South Livermore Avenue
LIVERMORE, CALIFORNIA 94550
(925) 447-8941 Fax (925) 447-8941
www.retzlaffwinery.com

CONTAINS SULFITES
CA #04-3424 CA. No 2003

GOVERNMENT WARNING: (1) ACCORDING TO THE
SURGEON GENERAL, WOMEN SHOULD NOT DRINK
ALCOHOLIC BEVERAGES DURING PREGNANCY
BECAUSE OF THE RISK OF BIRTH DEFECTS. (2)
CONSUMPTION OF ALCOHOLIC BEVERAGES
IMPAIRS YOUR ABILITY TO DRIVE A CAR OR OPERATE
MACHINERY, AND MAY CAUSE HEALTH PROBLEMS

08216   00007

Retzlaff Estate Winery
1356 S. Livermore Avenue
Livermore, CA 94550
(925) 447-8941

Website:
www.retzlaffwinery.com
Email:
retzlaffwinery@gmail.com

- Tasting room: Tuesday–Friday, noon–2; weekends, noon–4:30; $5 tasting fee (waived with purchase)

- Established: 1986

- Owner/winemaker: Robert Taylor

- Annual production: 3,000 cases

- Varieties: Sauvignon Blanc, Chardonnay, Merlot, and Cabernet Sauvignon—all estate grown and organic

- Wine club: Futures program

Fourteen Acres of Organic,
Estate-Grown Grapes

*R*obert and Gloria Taylor had little interest in wine, that is, until they lived in Germany and France, where Robert studied chemistry and discovered a culture where wine is a part of daily life.

After returning to America in 1975, the Taylors purchased an old farm on the outskirts of Livermore. Robert Taylor explained that they were merely looking for a quiet, pastoral place to call home. The centerpiece of the storybook homestead is a sun-dappled classic ranch house built in 1881 with its turn-of-the-century barns, water tower, and machine sheds. An inviting, tree-shrouded lawn fronts the board-and-batten tasting room.

Taylor remembers that they had no intention of growing grapes or becoming winemakers when they bought the property. "But, my wife, Gloria, who recently passed on, was a real visionary and an adventuresome sort. She couldn't stand seeing our land stay idle and so one day she announced, 'Let's plant some grapes!'"

In the beginning, they grew Grey Riesling, which was the top seller in the region thirty years ago. But the variety eventually fell out of favor and they grafted over to Semillon, Sauvignon Blanc, Chardonnay, Cabernet, and Merlot.

The road to Retzlaff Winery

When the Taylors segued into commercial winemaking in 1986, theirs was the sixth post-Prohibition winery to open its doors in Livermore Valley. They wanted to name their new winery Taylor Cellars, but the name was already taken. Instead, they chose Retzlaff in honor of Gloria's maiden name. Today, their fourteen acres of estate-grown grapes are all certified organic.

Bob Taylor pours a barrel sample for a guest.

Taylor says with reverence, "Gloria's vision for our winery was to create a place in Livermore Valley where people could come and share ideas, bring a picnic, and enjoy some wine, similar to what she saw in coffee shops in rural Germany. Her vision has become a reality here at Retzlaff Vineyards and has also contributed to a special homey spirit throughout the Livermore Valley wine region."

The grounds at Retzlaff are ideal for picnics.

Taylor says of his winemaking philosophy, "When you're

Gazebo outside of Retzlaff's tasting room

making wine and you get overly concerned about what to do, you have to remind yourself that people were making wine since before Christ—and they made it just fine in goat skins and clay pots. So even with all our modern technology the goal is to keep the process simple. I have seen cases where heroic measures were taken to correct what was thought to be a flawed wine when in fact it was just fine and should have been left alone."

He believes that chemistry can save winemakers from making some fundamental mistakes, but for him, the bottom line is that, "great wine is not made with technology—the best tool in a winery is your mouth."

Taylor's Semillon is a heavy producer. "On its own it's just an average varietal, but when we mix it with our Sauvignon Blanc, the two blended together become far superior to either on their own. Both whites and reds do quite well here, particularly Bordeaux varietals. They really like the cool nights and warm days."

Rather than making up names or using terms such as "meritage," Taylor simply puts on the labels what's in the bottle: if it's 30 percent Semillon, that's what the label says. "That way, our customers learn what it is that they like," he says. "And that's another advantage of estate bottling—the consumer knows exactly where the grapes came from. If they like it they know where they can buy the same wine the next year."

According to Taylor, Merlots do especially well in Livermore and tend to be rather soft, with lower tannins than Merlot made from grapes grown in Calistoga's volcanic soils. "Our Merlot ages extremely well, but it's also very drinkable as a young wine." The Livermore Valley is graced with a gravelly loam soil that Taylor thinks is just tremendous.

Rather than running a wine club, Retzlaff offers barrel futures. Once a wine is released, they host a party. The barrel investors enjoy the festivities and pick up their cases of wine. An added bonus of visiting the winery's tasting room is the enchanting nineteenth-century farmstead setting.

As I said goodbye, Taylor smiled as he attributed the family's success as growers and winemakers to his wife's vision and their loyal employees, especially Retzlaff's longtime field manager, José Hernandez, "who takes exquisite care of the vineyard."

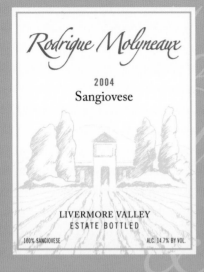

Rodrigue Molyneaux
Vineyard & Winery
3053 Marina Avenue
Livermore, CA 94550
925.443.1998

Website: www.rmwinery.com
Email: info@rmwinery.com
Facebook and Twitter

- Ce Tasting room: Weekends 12:30–5:00; $5 tasting fee (waived with purchase)

- Ce Established: 2004

- Ce Owners: Garry Rodrigue (winemaker) and Nancy Rodgrigue

- Ce Annual production: 2,000 cases

- Ce Varieties: Estate-grown Cabernet Sauvignon, Barbera, Sangiovese, Pinot Bianco, Port, Nebbiolo; Pinot Niro, Livermore Valley American Viticultural Area (AVA) Primitivo, Rosé

- Ce Wine club: Wineaux Wine Club

What Italy Tastes Like…

The nearby Lawrence Livermore National Laboratory is legendary for its top-secret military defense and counterterrorism projects, but I suspect it might just operate a clandestine incubator for aspiring winemakers on the side. Many local wineries are owned and operated by retired Livermore Lab research scientists, who all admit to first getting the enology bug and learning the craft while still employed at the lab. I can think of ten off the top of my head, and there are more out there.

One local vintner commented, "Without a doubt, the Livermore Valley wine industry is home to more over-educated growers and producers holding PhDs than any other American Viticultural Area."

Canadian-born Garry Rodrigue first embarked on his winemaking path while employed as a PhD research scientist at Livermore Lab and subsequently as a UC Davis professor of applied science. That's where the self-taught Rodrigue honed his insights into the art of growing and processing. "As a professor, I had access to the university's extensive wine library and the enology department," he recalled. "I also received lots of assistance from professionals in barreling, chemistry, and processing, as well as through winemaking seminars."

Garry and Nancy Rodrigue

Photo courtesy of Annie Tao Photography

About twelve years ago, Rodrigue confesses, he and his wife, Nancy, got "caught up in the wine renaissance that was sweeping Livermore Valley." The county was offering economic incentives to plant grapes; the Wente family and the county had a plan to steer the ideally suited region back into wine growing. "At the time," he recalls, "if you went before the water board and said you wanted water for grapes, you got your water!"

Fall at Rodrigue Molyneaux Winery

Nancy Rodgrigue, who was an instructor at nearby Las Positas College at the time, explained that the subsequent proliferation of Livermore Valley grape growers was followed by a wave of new wineries. "We've been here thirty-five years. When we first arrived, there

were only four, maybe five wineries in the entire valley. Wine soon became part of our life, and we loved visiting the local wineries."

In 1997, the couple bought an old farm, complete with an array of outbuildings and machine sheds, and planted their vineyard a year later. They opened their winery in 2004 following Rodrigue's retirement. His wife chuckled as she noted that their first tasting room was a simple, open-air affair, directly in front of the barrel room.

Garry Rodrigue praises the camaraderie of the valley's agricultural community. "I can't speak highly enough about the Wente family," he says, recalling the time he asked his neighbors if they could transport water to his property. "'No problem,'" they said, and the next day they brought over a trencher. A day later we had water!" Today, Wente Vineyards manages the Rodrigue Molyneaux vineyards, and Rodrigue works very closely with Wente's manager throughout the growing and harvesting process.

The key aspect of making a great bottle of wine, Rodrigue says, "comes from the vineyard." The couple proudly notes that more than half of their grapes are homegrown—with the remainder sourced nearby and from neighboring farms.

"You see lots of Cabs, Sirah, Sangiovese, Barbera, and Rhone varieties throughout the Livermore Valley—and they all do really well here," Rodrigue says. "I especially like big reds." The Livermore Valley's growing environment has many similarities to Tuscany, he explains, and that's why they and many others specialize in Italian style varietals and full-bodied blends. Dry daytime heat and cool nights, coupled with the rocky soil, create the perfect environment.

The tasting room functions as their primary source of sales, but the wine club is an equally essential aspect of the winery's operation and income. Rodrigue Molyneaux sponsors celebratory events for their wine club members, including Hot August Nights, Taste of Tuscany, and a popular annual harvest picnic. Three times a year, the winery distributes three bottles (including two new releases) to its wine club members, as well as offering special tastings and discounts.

They also offer a popular series of wine education classes, including Flavors in Wine, Vineyard to Bottle, and Wine Tasting.

"People can always tell a Rodrigue Molyneaux wine," Nancy says. "I am not exactly sure what it is, but there's something unique and distinctive about our wines' flavors."

Beyond the quest for distinctive wines, Nancy explains that the winery's shady gardens entice people to return to Rodrigue Molyneaux. "Many people buy a bottle and love to sit for a couple of hours on the grass, gazing at the vineyard and the horses next door. I think we are unique to Livermore in that way."

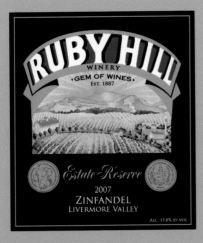

Ruby Hill Winery
400 Vineyard Avenue
Pleasanton, CA 94566
(925) 931-9463

Website: www.rubyhillwinery.net
Email: info@rubyhillwinery.net
Facebook

- Tasting room: 11–5:30 daily and by appointment;
  $5 tasting fee (waived with purchase)

- Established: 1887, re-established 2008

- Majority owner: Mike Callahan
  Winemaker: Chris Graves

- Annual production: 10,000 cases

- Varieties: Chardonnay, Sauvignon Blanc, Pinot Grigio,
  Cabernet, Rosé, Zinfandel, Petite Sirah, Sangiovese,
  Barbera, Merlot, Cabernet Sauvignon, Port, and more

- Wine club: Gem Society

The Gem of Wines

*R*uby Hill, one of Livermore Valley's oldest wineries, has morphed into one of the region's newest and most sophisticated Mediterranean-style facilities.

Ruby Hill (named after the rich red soil) first opened its cellar doors in 1887 and quickly grew to become one of the valley's largest growers and producers. The winery maintained more than 400 acres under cultivation and shipped approximately 400,000 gallons of wine annually.

According to present-owner Mike Callahan, "Ruby Hill made it through Prohibition selling Sacramental wine, but ultimately went broke and closed in the 1970s." The eye-catching, circa-1887 brick winery building remained dormant and decaying until Callahan purchased a 150-acre portion of the Ruby Hill estate and refurbished the historic brick building and new Palm Event Center.

Subsequently, Callahan built an opulent, Mediterranean-style reincarnated Ruby Hill Winery and Casa Real Event Center next door and opened for business in 2008.

Callahan, who was born and raised in nearby Castro Valley, shared his philosophy and Ruby Hill's mission to be a California boutique winery with a little hint of Italy. The winery's goal, he explained is to "set Livermore Valley on the map with some incredible wines." A business model of volume production (10,000-case annual production presently with an upward trend planned for an eventual output of 50,000 or more) allows Ruby Hill to "purchase the finest equipment and hire the best talent, such as winemaker Chris Graves."

"It's all about family, friends, food, and good wine," Graves said, summing up his passion for the wine industry. In fact, it was his family that foresaw Graves' future as a winemaker: when he was just sixteen years old, his parents suggested he consider a career in the field.

After completing two AA degrees, Graves entered UC Davis's enology and viticulture program and became an intern at Wente

Vineyards. Immediately upon graduation, he was hired there as an enologist and was eventually promoted to winemaker at Wente's Tamas Estates winery. Two years later, he was hired by Mike Callahan to become Ruby Hill's winemaker.

Ruby Hill Winery

According to Graves, Ruby Hill specializes in "hands-on winemaking of the highest degree, with a focus on Zinfandel and Petite Sirah." He notes they also have a passion for Italian and many other varietals.

Ruby Hill produces approximately 75 percent estate-bottled wines and those from locally grown grapes, as well as a wide array of California-coastal-sourced grapes. Their blends include Super Tuscan and a Bordeaux style.

The fine balance between the science and art of winemaking is an integral part of

Winemaker Chris Graves

most winemakers' experience, and Graves believes it's important to have an equilibrium between the two sides of the winemaking experience. "There is the talent and the artistic understanding and appreciation for wine flavor and balance—which is something that you can't always learn," he adds. "But certainly a full understanding of the winemaking process, the biochemistry and microbiology, is an integral part of staying consistent and making good quality wine, as well as an understanding of the fermentation process, inside and out."

But, he adds, what it really comes down to is when you taste the wine. "We can sometimes pick up changes in wines with our noses before chemistry can."

The wines produced at Ruby Hill are typically a rich California fruit-forward style. They tend to be intense with a good balance between fruit, oak, acidity, and tannins. Graves prefers lively, palatable, and approachable wines. "For the most part, I enjoy well-balanced bigger wines," he says, "but definitely, no wimpy wines."

The opportunity to head up the new Ruby Hill Winery was a dream come true for Graves. "It is a joy to be involved in hands-on viticulture and winemaking at Ruby Hill Winery," he says with a smile, "where I am able to maximize my potential in both the art and science of winemaking!"

Chris lives on the property with his family and keeps a close eye on his wines.

The Singing Winemaker
5143 Tesla Road
Livermore, CA 94550
(925) 606-9463

Website:
www.teslavintners.com
Email:
patty@teslavintners.com

- Tasting room: Friday–Sunday, noon–5;
  $5 tasting fee (waived with purchase)

- Established: 2004

- Owners/winemaker: Steve (winemaker) and Karen Powell

- Annual production: 1,400 cases

- Varieties: Melody (Cabernet, Merlot, Petite Sirah),
  Harmony (Petite Sirah, Merlot), Karen's Kisses late
  harvest Zinfandel, Symphony, and Sherzando. Sparkling
  wine: peach, raspberry, and almond; Tawny Port; and
  Framboise

*Celebrating Truth, Beauty, and Goodness
through Wine, Music, and Art*

The story of Tesla Vintners and The Singing Winemaker is a tale of local boy makes good. Steve Powell, born and raised in Livermore, graduated from the local community college in communications and computer science. In 1985 he and his first wife bought the Tesla Road property and the century-old farmstead that today houses his Tesla Vintners tasting room.

"At the time, my wife wanted a horse ranch, so we put in stalls and an arena," he recalls. "In addition to horses we had cows and goats and pigs. When my marriage went away so did the animals, but I wound up with the property."

At the time, the wine industry was just starting to boom and Powell's curiosity was piqued. He recalls that when he purchased the property an average of 300 cars a day would putter past. By 2003, a traffic study reported more than 17,000 vehicles a day. Life had changed on Tesla Road, and his home was no longer an ideal residence. It was, however, perfect for a commercial venture.

When the owners of Big White House Winery and Little Valley Winery voiced an interest in starting the valley's first community tasting room at his property—just a stone's throw from the Wente and Concannon wineries—he was ready to rock and roll. In fall 2004, Livermore Valley's first community tasting room opened under a tent with four wineries represented: Little Valley, Big White House, Fenestra, and Thomas Coyne.

Powell had never made wine, he says, "but I long enjoyed wine tasting and the lifestyle." The energy and enthusiasm of the winemakers was infectious, and before long he was training under Coyne and another winemaker friend. Powell says he's very comfortable operating a boutique winery, "because it's really a social thing—as much about art and music as wine." Thus, their tagline became: Tesla Vintners, Celebrating Truth, Beauty, and Goodness Through Wine, Music, and Art.

When they opened for business, Powell remembers, most of the area's boutique tasting rooms were funky and minimalist. The group decided to raise the bar and install granite countertops and feature lots of local art. "The intent was to meld wine, art, and music together," he says. A musician himself, Powell is the namesake of The Singing Winemaker label. "I started singing and playing music in the tasting room and for the first three or four years it was swamped."

Eventually, the other wineries evolved and developed divergent business models, moving on to establish their own tasting rooms. Today, Tesla Vintners showcases The Singing Winemaker and two other wineries: Miramont Estate Vineyard, which is a central valley winemaker, and Marr Vineyards, which sources grapes from Ukiah, Tehama, and Yolo Counties.

When Powell started his commercial winemaking venture, he knew he couldn't compete with the numerous

Photos by Thomas C. Wilmer

Outdoor seating at Tesla Vintners

Old water tower on Tesla Vintners Property

valley vintners making individual varieties such as Cabernets and Merlot, so he decided to specialize in blends and sweet wines. He believes many winemakers create blends out of wines that, on their own, would not be up to par. "I thought, if they can make great blends from not so great wines, I can make really great blends from superior wines."

Powell's first blend was a very complex assemblage called Patty's Passion, named after his tasting room manager. "At the conclusion of every day, Patty would blend whatever wines were opened to see what she could come up with." One of Patty's blends blew Powell away. "Patty," he told her, "you're going to create our first blend!" The complex array included Syrah, Grenache, and Petite Sirah. "We wound up with a superb wine that won a bunch of awards. Unfortunately, it was so complex we could never replicate it again—we sure learned our lesson!"

Powell's present offerings are musical-themed blends such as Symphony and Harmony. Melody, a combination of Cab Merlot and Petite Sirah, is his flagship wine, along with Harmony, a blend of Petite Sirah and Merlot. Powell has discovered a niche with his appetite for sweet wines. "Three years in a row I had the only white wines in *Diablo Magazine*'s Tri-Valley Top Ten list, and they were all sweet wines!" His Framboise is so popular that the superstore BevMo! carries it.

"Our philosophy is to provide the public with a full spectrum of tasting options," he says, "from bold, fruit-forward reds to soft and smooth old-world-style wines." Powell's goal is to make wines that appeal to whoever walks in the door. If you pay him a visit, you might just find something that you really love and want to take home.

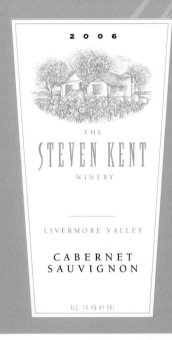

The Steven Kent Winery
5443 Tesla Road
Livermore, CA 94550
(925) 243-6440

Website: www.stevenkent.com
Email:
winesales@stevenkent.com
Facebook

- Tasting room: Daily, noon–4:30; flights available wine-only and with pairings
- Established: 1999
- Owner: Steven Kent Mirassou
  Winemakers: Steven Mirassou and Claude Bobba
- Annual production: 7,000 cases, plus 15,000 cases for Ritz-Carlton
- Varieties: Cabernet Sauvignon, Chardonnay, Cabernet Franc, Sauvignon Blanc, Sangiovese, Barbera
- Wine clubs: Future Release Program and Collector's Circle

Wines for Those Who Know

*M*y entrée to fine wine was a memorable bottle of Mirassou Chardonnay shared with a friend at a Santa Cruz diner back in 1976. Who knows? If it weren't for the Mirassou family, right now I might be in the midst of writing a book about breweries and brewmeisters.

Steven Kent Mirassou should rightfully be a champagne maker, as he nearly bursts with a profound passion for fine wines and the art of winemaking. He didn't stumble into viticulture by happenstance. In a sense, his path was pre-ordained, as he is a member of America's oldest winemaking family who's been in the business since 1852 (see section on La Rochelle Winery).

Until the mid-1940s, the Mirassous produced bulk wine. Later, in the mid-60s, Mirassou's father, uncle, and cousins expanded the San Jose-based operation from a regional producer into a nationally distributed brand. In 1984, his father split off from the family business and started Ivan Tamás winery. "Moving the winery operation to Livermore in the late 1980s was serendipitous for all of us," Mirassou says. "My dad and Ivan came here at the invitation of Eric Wente, who offered invaluable winemaking and administrative support for their Ivan Tamás wines."

Their ability to utilize the built-in infrastructure of Wente's processing facility was an added benefit. Wente had concentrated for

Photo courtesy of *The Independent Magazine*

Winemaker Steven Kent Mirassou shares his love for Cab with guests.

Steven Kent Tasting Room at night

decades on white wines, and Mirassou says he and his father realized there was a great opportunity to establish high-end Cabernet production because Livermore Valley is an ideal place to grow Bordeaux varieties.

With a focused vision and an investment of time and money in the vineyard, they were confident that high-quality Cabernets could be made here. "We were also very impressed with the collegial and supportive local winemaker community," Mirassou recalls.

In 2003, the Gallo Corporation purchased the Mirassou brand, along with inventory and rights to the Mirassou name. Neither Steven Mirassou nor his dad have used the Mirassou name since they left the company in 1984.

Mirassou's first wine love was—and still is—Cabernet, and he believes it produces the best red wine in the world. Mirassou strategically positioned the Steven Kent Winery as a Bordeaux house, producing the classic Bordeaux varieties, all grown at the nearby Ghielmetti Vineyards. He also produces some Rhones, including Mourvedre and Petite Sirah.

Like a persuasive evangelist, Mirassou raves about Livermore Valley's amazing Cabernet and its ideal growing conditions. With the western boundary of the AVA only about twenty miles from the San Francisco Bay, "We have warm days with excellent ripening effect, but we also receive the cool marine air almost every afternoon," he says, "and thus the ideal conditions to produce superbly balanced, complex Bordeaux varietals."

What they are accomplishing at Steven Kent, Mirassou says, is the creation of a world-class Cabernet from a non-Napa appellation. "Napa grows great Cabernet, but it's by no means the only place [to grow it], as evidenced by Paso Robles, Bordeaux, and Livermore Valley."

In Livermore, Mirassou says, "we tend to make wines that are densely fruited; you can tell by the nose that there are layers and layers going on. Livermore wines have a nice rich and full mid-palate, and the tannins tend to come toward the end, as opposed to Napa cabs, which generally have tannins running all the way through." Mirassou also crafts Sangiovese and Barbera and believes that the Italian varietals are equally suited to the local *terroir*.

All of the final blendings and most of the Cabernet barrel selections are done by Mirassou, while his winemaking team handles production up to malolactic fermentation. "Once the wines are stable, I start making mock blends until I really like the wine," he explains. "From there, the blends are put together, re-barreled, and released one to two years later."

The winemaking team, headed by Claude Bobba and Tom Stutz, oversees both Steven Kent and La Rochelle wines. Bobba and Mirassou work together to formulate the specifications for all Steven Kent wines, while Stutz oversees La Rochelle's production. This, Mirassou says, is why it's sometimes hard to track him down. "I work closely with the vineyard manager at Ghielmetti Vineyards, sell the extra fruit to local wineries, write all the marketing materials and technical sheets, do the blogs, help with Facebook pages, Twitter updates, and websites, and go on the road to sell our wine in California and Florida."

He says his goal is to produce world-class, ultra-premium Cabernet and Chardonnay wines in small, handcrafted lots from the best grapes Livermore Valley has to offer. Given his passion, dedication, and stellar team, I'd say he's well on his way.

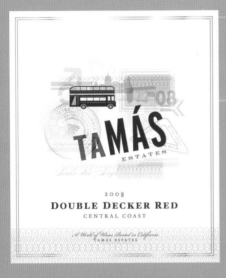

Tamás Estates
5565 Tesla Road
Livermore, CA 94550
(925) 456-2380

Website:
www.tamasestates.com
Email:
tastingroom@tamasestates.com

- Tasting room: 11–4:30 daily; $5 tasting fee

- Established: 1984

- Owners: The Wente family

- Annual production: 60,000 cases

- Varieties: Pinot Grigio and Zinfandel. Barbera and Sangiovese; Blends: Double Decker Red, Vino Rosso, Andiamo, Toscanelli, Il Viaggio, Fiorente, Sorrento and Prima

- Wine club: Salute Wine Club

A World of Wines Rooted in California

*I*ván Tamás Fuezy and Steve Mirassou founded Tamás Estates in 1984. Steve Mirassou's son, Steven Kent Mirassou, explains, "My dad and Iván came here at the invitation of Eric Wente, as he offered invaluable winemaking and administrative support and the benefits of Wente's built-in infrastructure."

Carolyn Wente remembers that during their stewardship, Fuezy and Mirassou were crafting "these beautiful, fresh California-style, fruit-forward wines that were so clean and crisp—exceptional everyday table wines." The Wente family became actively involved when Carolyn and her two brothers Eric and Philip were asked to blend and bottle some of the wines. "We said sure, because custom winemaking for other people is one of our specialties." The Wente family eventually broadened their relationship with Tamás Estates to include marketing the wines, as well. When Mirassou and Fuezy retired, they sold the winery to the Wentes, and the family has operated

The tasting room of Tamás Estates

it ever since. "Their original winemaking style evolved to become the wines that we produce today," she says.

Tamás Estates wines, she explains, are meant to offer an exploration of the world of wine. "It's your ticket to Italy, to France, it's your ticket to Croatia—if you think that's where Zinfandel originated." Tamás Estates' varieties may offer a veritable trip around the world, but these adventurous wines are all grown in their estate vineyards in Livermore Valley, San Francisco Bay, and Arroyo Seco, Monterey, appellations—and they have a distinctive California flair.

Fifth-generation winegrower and winemaker Karl Wente adds, "Since all of the cultivars are estate grown we can control the vineyard and farm for the exact flavors that we are looking for." He carries on his ancestors' style of a hands-on approach to winemaking. "There is no substitute for time spent in the field, and successful winemaking is a blend of insight combined with hands-on experience."

Wines at Tamás Estates

For twenty years the Wente's have maintained a focus on producing quality wines that are very affordable for the consumer. They're able to achieve this, Karl explains, "because we have the advantage of control over the grapes we produce, and equally important, we've owned the land for many years." He points out that those who've entered the industry in recent years have often paid exorbitant land prices—and their commensurately high overhead is reflected in higher retail price points. "Our family, from my great grandfather on down, has believed in passing along to the consumer quality, fruit-forward wines at reasonable prices."

An integral aspect of Tamás Estates' operation, and throughout all of the Wente family's other wineries, is a dedicated commitment to sustainable growing practices. Karl Wente's elders, Phil and Eric, served individual terms as president of the non-profit Wine Institute and were intimately involved in developing the organization's Code of Sustainable Winegrowing Practices. The family's passion for innovation and experimentation has been a hallmark, Karl says, "since we introduced the first varietally labeled wines back in the 1930s."

"Our wines really appeal to the next generation of wine drinkers," Carolyn says. Even Tamás Estates' packaging is hip and cutting-edge. "They love our Pinot Grigio and especially our recently released Double Decker Red," a blend of global varietals that invites wine drinkers to *hop on the bus* and expand their wine experiences. The wine, with its passport-inspired label, invites those who enjoy it to escape, relax, unwind, and even plan a trip or reminisce about a past one.

In addition to the popular Double Decker Red, another hot ticket item is the super Tuscan-style blend of Sangiovese and Cabernet, as well as their Zinfandel. And Tamás Estates has ventured into new territory with the recent addition of a Pinot Noir.

Tamás Estates' popular varietals thrive in California's Mediterranean climate, and their Pinot Grigio, grown in Monterey County's cool climate, is light, aromatic, and crisp with full flavors of grapefruit and citrus. "Our red wines, sourced from the Livermore Valley, absolutely thrive in the perfect conditions of the gravelly soils and climate influenced by the San Francisco Bay breezes," Carolyn says. Visit Tamás Estates and experience these wines, which are crafted to be approachable and food-friendly, with prices that lend themselves to everyday enjoyment.

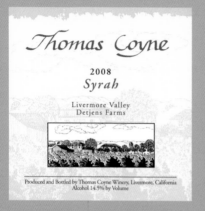

Thomas Coyne Winery
51 East Vallecitos Road
Livermore, CA 94550
(925) 373-6541

Website:
thomascoynewinery.com

- Tasting room: Weekends, noon–5; Additional tasting room in Blacksmith Square: Friday, 3–6; weekends, noon–6

- Established: 1989

- Owners: Emilie and Thomas Coyne (winemaker)

- Annual production: 3,000–4,000 cases

- Varieties: Viognier, Mourvedre, Petite Sirah, Pinot Blanc, Merlot, Cabernet Sauvignon, Cabernet Franc, and Petit Verdot

Elegant Wine in a Rustic Setting

rench engineer Alexander Duvall made his fortune in South America and then settled in Livermore Valley, where he opened the legendary Chateau Bellevue in 1881. He was one of the valley's pioneer vintners.

Duvall employed a visionary array of environmentally friendly elements in his new winery. He utilized the thermal mass of brick walls nearly two feet thick, excavated the backside of his processing facility seven feet into the hillside, and installed only north-facing windows to avoid sunlight infiltration. He also utilized gravity-fed chutes to transport the juice from the upper floor to redwood tanks below.

More than 120 years later, Duvall's winery lives on under the stewardship of Thomas and Emilie Coyne. Tucked into a sleepy hillside, with panoramic vistas of grape fields and Mount Diablo on the far horizon, the ancient winery remains frozen in time with its original plaster ceilings and gravity chutes through the upper floor. The patina on the vintage wooden barn doors is testament to a time long vanished.

Thomas Coyne is somewhat of a pioneer in his own right, as his winemaking history dates back to 1969 in western New York. A

Chateau Bellevue c. 1881

Photo courtesy of Steven F. Kelly

Thomas Coyne bottles his wine

chemical engineering graduate of Penn State, Coyne began crafting homemade wine with Native American Catawba and Concord
varietals. "Later on, we added some locally grown French hybrids,
as well as California lug-box Petite Sirah and Zinfandel that we'd
pick up at a farmers market in Patterson, New Jersey."

In 1977 Coyne went to work at Clorox Company's Pleasanton
operation. There, he met some local home winemakers, including rising star Kent Rosenblum, who started his own commercial
operation around 1978. In 1988 Coyne bailed from corporate life
and started as full-time cellar master at Rosenblum Cellars. A year
later, he launched Thomas Coyne Winery utilizing Rosenblum's
crush facilities.

Coyne rented the old Chateau Bellevue winery facility in 1994,
and he's been contentedly crafting his fine wines there ever since.

Since starting his Livermore Valley winery, Coyne has spent
endless hours sharing his knowledge and offering use of his facilities to numerous neophyte winemakers. He never uttered a word
about this to me, but his name comes up countless times in other
vintners' tales of how local winemakers helped them to learn and
understand the art of their craft.

Coyne focuses on Rhone and Bordeaux varietals. In his Rhone lexicon, he utilizes Viognier, Grenache, Syrah, and Mourvedre as single varietals. His blends include Quest, which is a combination of Grenache, Syrah, and Mourvedre, and a Rosé called Petite Quest.

He also uses all of the five classic Bordeaux grapes—Cabernet Sauvignon, Cabernet Franc, Malbec, Petit Verdot, and Merlot. Coyne produces three distinctive Merlots sourced from various California appellations and is passionate about his quest to make the finest possible. He also offers a variety of Petite Sirahs, a Portuguese Port, a white Chardonnay Port named Sweet Emilie in honor of his wife, and dessert wines, including one from a late-harvest Viognier.

Striving to produce fruit-forward styles that are indicative of the particular varietals, Coyne believes it is equally important to maintain good relationships with the growers. "If we have long-term access to the same fruit we know how the grower performs and therefore the specific characteristics of the grapes—and our goal is to extend that into our high-quality wines."

He crafts no "wimpy wines" and implements extensive barrel aging. For the whites, he practices all barrel fermentation with sur lie aging and then bottles after five or six months. For his reds, he barrel ages from eighteen to twenty-four months using a blend of French, Hungarian, and American oak. "We vary that depending on the kind of wine we're making," he says.

For some of his lighter red blends, Coyne explains, he won't use any new oak, but rather oak that's two to three years old. Whereas on the other side of the spectrum, he will age Petite Sirahs in one- or two-year-old oak because he's looking for a "bigger expression." He favors French oak for Cabs but American oak for Petite Sirah.

When you drive out to the historic winery, you may just have the honor of meeting one of Livermore Valley's modern-day wine industry icons—and you'll definitely have the chance to sip some awesome wines.

Wente Vineyards
(925) 456-2300

The Estate Tasting Room
5565 Tesla Road
Livermore, CA 94550
(925) 456-2305

The Vineyard Tasting Room
5050 Arroyo Road
Livermore, CA 94550
(925) 456-2405

Website: wentevineyards.com
Email: tastingroom@wentevineyards.com

- The Estate Tasting Room: 11–4:30 daily; Complimentary flight & $5-10 for Small Lot and Nth Degree flights; Winery tours daily: 11am, 1, 2, & 3pm
- The Vineyard Tasting Room: 11–6:30 daily; $5-$10 flights
- Established: 1883
- Owners: The Wente family; Winemaker: Karl D. Wente
- Annual production: 300,000 cases
- Varieties: Cabernet Sauvignon, Merlot, Pinot Noir, Syrah, Chardonnay, Sauvignon Blanc, and Riesling (Nth Degree wines include Chardonnay, Merlot, Syrah, Cabernet Sauvignon, and Pinot Noir)
- Wine clubs: Club Wente and The Nth Degree Club

Family Owned. Estate Grown.
Sustainably Farmed.

The Wente story has as much to do with its amazing history as its present status as one of the country's premier wineries. Founded in 1883, it is America's oldest, continuously operated, family-owned winery.

Carl Heinrich Wente emigrated from Hanover, Germany, around 1870 and came to America in search of two half-brothers reportedly living in Illinois or Minnesota. According to Carl's son Ernest in a 1969 interview, his father never found his brothers. He drifted out West to Kansas and then on to Lake County, northern California, where he worked as a ranch hand before having the good fortune to meet and gain employment with Prussian immigrant Charles Krug.

Apprenticed in the art of winemaking in Germany, Krug became Napa Valley's first commercial vintner in 1858 and established his St. Helena winery in 1861. The thirty-five-year-old Krug taught Carl Wente the art of winemaking, and he quickly became Krug's cellar master.

Having mastered the nuances of winemaking and motivated to make it on his own, Wente realized that Livermore Valley was California's premier growing region. Its warm days, cool nights,

Sustainably farmed vines at Wente Vineyards

and gravelly, well-drained soils were ideal for growing grapes. He purchased forty-seven acres and founded his Livermore winery in 1883 in partnership with two local doctors, whom he eventually bought out.

In 1918, Wente's sons, Ernest and Herman, joined the business. Ernest managed the vineyards and Herman acted as winemaker. When Ernest retired, he passed the reigns to his only son, Karl. In 1977, Karl passed away and his sons, Eric and Phil, took the helm. They were soon joined by their sister Carolyn. Continuing the century-and-a-quarter legacy, the fourth generation of the Wente family—Eric, Philip, and Carolyn—and the fifth generation—Christine and Karl D. Wente—manage the winery.

When Carl Heinrich Wente purchased his acreage in 1883, twenty acres were already planted with Zinfandel and some Charbono, Colombard, Mataro, and Grey Riesling, which Wente eventually grafted over to White Riesling. Plantings of Semillon and Sauvignon Blanc were later added. Wente received his Sauvignon cuttings from Louis Mel, who brought them from the famed Château d'Yquem winery in Sauternes, France.

From its inception, Carl Wente's winery was a bulk producer (onsite bottling of Wente-labeled wines was introduced after prohibition). His wine was shipped in bulk and bottled by the Napa & Sonoma Wine Company (of which Wente was co-owner), and sold to Beaulieu Vineyards, Gundlach-Bundschu in Sonoma, and Italian Swiss Colony, as well as a handful of wine merchants.

Wente's wines were widely recognized by fellow winemakers and discerning industry experts as among California's finest. At the 1915 Panama Pacific International Exposition in San Francisco, Carl Heinrich Wente reportedly remarked, "I am probably the proudest man here at the fair because I have just won four gold medals. But none of them are in my name!" Only a handful of people knew that the award-winning Wente wines were presented to the public under Beaulieu's and other Napa and Sonoma labels—and those wineries walked away with the gold medals. In

1918, Wente and his family created the Wente Brothers company name (but did not release a Wente-labeled wine until 1934) followed by a Valle de Oro label, C.H. Wente & Sons, and the current Wente Vineyards label.

During Prohibition, Wente's close friendship with Georges de Latour of Beaulieu Vineyards served as a Godsend for the family operation. Carolyn Wente says, "The de Latour family was Catholic, and my grandfather annually supplied 30,000 gallons of Sweet Sauternes to Beaulieu that was subsequently sold to the Catholic Church as sacramental wine, and that's what kept our winery in business." The Wentes also shipped grapes by railcar for the East Coast home winemaker market and increased their cattle-and-hay operation to carry them through Prohibition.

Following that era, the California market was dominated by blended wines, and the family knew they needed to distinguish themselves. Across America, individual varieties were labeled Chablis, Burgundy, and Sauterne after their historic Old Country roots. The Wente family made the bold move to introduce the first varietally labeled wines—something that had never been done before in California. Wente was the first winery to varietally label Sauvignon Blanc, Grey Riesling, and Chardonnay—commonly known until then as White Burgundy. Carolyn says proudly, "Today more than half of the world's wines are varietally labeled."

The Wente family was the first to introduce Chardonnay to California and America. Carolyn recalls that her grandfather, Ernest, was in the first graduating class of UC Davis and was the second student to enroll in the newly opened agricultural university in 1908. Leon Bonnet, one of his professors from France, toured California's vineyards and was surprised by the complete absence of Chardonnay vines. Professor Bonnet realized that Livermore's soil and growing conditions were remarkably similar to the premier Chardonnay growing region of Burgundy, and he offered to secure cuttings from Montpellier, France, if Ernest Wente would plant them. Carolyn explains that her grandfather, an energetic nineteen-year-old at the time, enthusiastically agreed and planted his first Chardonnay vines in 1916. Even though Prohibition hit just a few years later, the Wente family continued to propagate more cuttings and increased the block. The Wentes released their first vintage-dated Chardonnay in 1936. "As late as 1960 my family owned one-third of all the Chardonnay planted in the entire state of California, and at the time it totaled a whopping seventy acres!" Carolyn says.

The Restaurant at Wente Vineyards

As Chardonnay's popularity burgeoned, the UC Davis viticultural department selected Wente's vines as the source Chardonnay for its nursery-

The Course at Wente Vineyards

vineyard, and today more than 80 percent of California's Chardonnay vines are Wente clones. Carolyn says, "It has grown to become the number-one selling white varietal in the United States and possibly the world."

Presently, all of Wente's grapes are estate grown and sustainably farmed on their two thousand acres in Livermore Valley and their one thousand acres in the Monterey County Arroyo Seco appellation. Wente family members, consistently among the top thirty wine growers and producers in California, have been unswerving industry trend setters. Their pioneering move into Monterey's Arroyo Seco back in 1961 happened a decade before the region exploded as one of the state's most favored growing regions. The Wentes adopted stainless steel fermentation tanks in the early

1960s and were the first to introduce mechanical harvesting, ahead of the curve in instituting sustainable practices throughout their business. They also produce and market an award-winning olive oil from their century-old trees, and the list goes on. In recent years, fourth-generation Wentes Eric, Philip, and Carolyn have defined Livermore Valley wine country as a regional destination with their fine wines, award-winning restaurant, championship golf course, and renowned summer concert series.

According to Carolyn, the Wente family winemaking philosophy is predicated on producing "beautifully balanced wines that are fruit forward, with the flavors being developed by the region in which they're grown." It's always been about wine that you can have on your table every night and enjoy, she says. Offering affordable wines is also important to the family. "And we firmly believe that you can make great wines that are sustainably farmed and reasonably priced." The Wente family's philosophy obviously works, as in addition to nationwide sales their wines are exported around the world to more than fifty countries, including Switzerland, Japan, Germany, and Canada, as well as the Caribbean.

The wine country experience, Carolyn says, is not just about going to a winery and tasting ten different wines. It's about having great food, being out in the country, and enjoying the vineyards, and that's an essential reason why they opened their restaurant. As a guest of the award-winning, trend-setting Wente family, you can enjoy great food and great wine in the Livermore Valley wine country setting.

*Additional source material from UC Berkeley Bancroft Library, Regional Oral History Office.

*Oral interview conducted by Ruth Teiser in 1969: Wine Making in the Livermore Valley by Ernest A. Wente.

Westover Vineyards,
Winery & Event Center
Palomares Vineyards
34329 Palomares Road
Castro Valley, CA 94552
(510) 537-3932

Website: www.westoverwinery.com
Email: westover@msn.com

- Tasting room: Weekdays, by appointment; weekends, noon–5

- Established: Westover Vineyards, Winery and Event Center, 1985; Palomares Vineyards, 2000

- Owners: William (Bill) Westover Smyth (winemaker) and Jill Ramie Smyth (wedding and spa director)

- Annual production: 2,500–3,000 cases

- Varieties: Chardonnay, Sauvignon Blanc, Pinot Grigio, Viognier, Riesling, Gewürztraminer, Cabernet Sauvignon, Cabernet Franc, Pinot Noir, Petite Sirah, Merlot, Zinfandel, Petit Verdot, Syrah, twenty-six different Ports, three champagnes, Rosé, Muscat, and Creme Sherry

- Amenities: Excellent wedding locale and corporate retreat venue with state-licensed private hair salon and massage facilities

- Wine club: Connoisseurs of Westover (COW) Club

At Westover, Winemaking Is Art

A must-stop destination in bucolic Palomares Canyon, the Westover Winery is also an event center and home to the Palomares Vineyards winery.

Winemaker Bill Smyth's life story is similar to most Livermore Valley winery owners in that it is multi-faceted and astounding.

Smyth honed his winemaking skills while training at the legendary Rosenblum Cellars in Alameda, along with stints at Hungarian, German, and South African wineries. In addition to Smyth's winemaking skills, he's also worked for the past twenty-nine years in the medical/surgical corporate field (with multiple certificates in surgery), not to mention his two-year stint on Wall Street, a year in South Africa with Shell Oil, and the time he worked in the former Yugoslavia. Along the way, he was also ordained a minister.

His wife, Jill, adds with a proud smile, "In addition to performing many of our wedding services, he also coordinates the weddings with me, and he's even been known to park a car or two."

Jill Smyth brings her own expertise to Westover Vineyards, including a past career with Ernst and Young Accounting and as

Ashley, Jill, and William Smyth in Vineyard's spa

Photo courtesy of *The Independent Magazine*

winemaker of her own Palo-mares wines. She serves as Director of the onsite Salon and Spa.

When I asked the Smyths to summarize their wine-making philosophies, I real-ized in retrospect that their answer was also a metaphor for their lives. "We look at winemaking as an art project. Every wine is like painting a picture, each one distinct and unique. Everything we

Event Center at Westover Winery

Thomas C. Wilmer

do, we approach with the attitude that we will never regret doing it. Never look back, and be sure to keep focused!"

The Smyths, along with assistant winemaker Scott Pearson, are proud of the fact that their grapes are crushed, fermented, aged, blended, filtered, and bottled on-site with their own equipment. "There are no trucks or other wineries bottling our wine," Bill Smyth proudly states.

When Westover Vineyards joined the Livermore Valley Wine-growers Association, there were less than ten member wineries. The Smyths purchased their stunning ten-acre Palomares Canyon property in 1985 and soon planted a three-acre Chardonnay and Pinot vineyard. Five years later, they started crafting their own wines and opened a tasting room. Today, Westover boasts the larg-est selection of wine, Port, Sherry, and sparkling wine in Livermore Valley.

The Smyths love Ports so much that they produce twenty-six varieties—the largest selection of any winery in America. They also produce three distinctive Grand Cuvee and Cuvee Close Champagnes, along with a Rosé sparkling wine, a Crème Sherry, and a Muscat (Jill's favorite).

In addition to their popular Cabernet Sauvignon, Syrah, Zinfandel, and Merlot, the most legendary Westover wine is their meritage, Je t'aime (French for "I love you"), a blend of Cabernet, Cabernet Franc, and Merlot.

Westover's seductive mountain setting, with a backdrop of lush green towering trees and ferns, is complete with a courtyard fountain and waterfall reception area—the centerpiece for most weddings held here (up to 200 guests). Westover offers the full array of ancillary wedding amenities, including a full-service salon and complete spa facilities. Their daughter, Ashley, is the on-site masseuse. The Smyths also offer custom wine labels that include wedding dates and pictures.

Sales and distribution are two of the most challenging aspects of operating a boutique winery. In addition to tasting room sales, weddings serve as a point of sale for Westover's wines—with the bonus that for many of the wedding participants, it is their first introduction to Westover and they subsequently become ardent wine club members.

Westover features both indoor and outdoor facilities. Bill's corporate background provided him with the insight to craft the ideal setting and amenities for productive meetings. Corporate groups enjoy al fresco lunch breaks adjacent to the waterfall in the picnic area. At the end of the day, the Smyths serve their wine and fine cheeses and, upon request, participants are offered barrel samplings of future vintages.

Special public and wine-club events are scheduled throughout the year, including the iconic Port & Cigars Under the Stars, which features wine tasting, live music, a Westover port glass, and appetizers of cheese and chocolate.

Westover is situated twenty-five minutes from the heart of the Tesla Road Wine Trail and almost exactly in the middle of the San Francisco Bay Area. Without a doubt, straying from the path to make the journey through magical Palomares Canyon is worth the time and effort, you'll be glad you did.

White Crane Winery
5405 Greenville Road
Livermore, CA 94550
(925) 455-8085

Website:
www.whitecranewinery.com
Email:
info@whitecranewinery.com

- Tasting room: Every day (except Tuesdays and Wednesdays), noon–4:30, and by appointment; $5 fee (waived with purchase)

- Established: May 2001

- Owners: A group of local investors including cofounder Nick Nardolillo, Winemakers Steve Burman, Nick Nardolillo, and Steve Ziganti

- Annual production: 3,000 cases

- Varieties: Cabernet Sauvignon, Cabernet Franc, Merlot, Zinfandel, Petite Sirah, Pinot Noir, Bordeaux blends, Chardonnay, Pinot Grigio, Portuguese Port, Chardonnay Port

- Amenities: Two on-site guest suites, ideal for wedding parties

- Wine club: White Crane Wine Club

Your Destination for Premium, Award-Winning Wines

*N*ick Nardolillo's Italian ancestry nurtured a lifelong love of wine and winemaking. He remembers often having a taste of wine as a kid at the dinner table. "Uncle Pete used to make the wine, and I will never forget him asking Grandma to get the chilled burgundy out of the fridge." The warmer it got, Nardolillo remembers, the more it tasted like gasoline. "Actually, it was a tad stronger than diesel fuel!" he jokes.

For Nardolillo, who grew up in nearby Castro Valley, wine remains an integral part of his family life.

After a stint in the Air Force working on intelligence projects at the National Security Agency, earning two teaching credentials, and running a very successful Bay Area advertising agency for twenty years, Nardolillo knew it was time to follow his passion and get back to his roots. In 2000, he and a partner purchased an existing vineyard property on Greenville Road.

One moonlit night not long after he bought the property, Nardolillo was walking through the fields, thinking about what to name his winery. "All of a sudden, a white crane swooped close

Nick Nardolillo, Debbie Francis, and Dino Nardolillo take time to make a toast

Tasting room at White Crane Winery

overhead, backlit by the full moon just like ET, and landed on a nearby fence post." Thus was born White Crane Winery.

In 2005 his business partner decided to leave the winery business and Nardolillo went looking for local investors. The investors he found are passionate about wine and are involved in everything from harvest to wine making, bottling and running the tasting room.

White Crane's operation has as much to do with providing a venue for great musical entertainment and festive parties as it does with crafting a wide variety of small-lot, limited-production, ultra-premium "Ferrari" wines. Customers enjoy the fun summer concert series hosted at the winery, and, with a big grin on his face, Nardolillo comments that the annual grape stomping party is one of his favorite events.

The winery provides guests with a hearty breakfast and then sends them out to harvest grapes. When they return to the lawn area, a pedicure station awaits them. The men wash the women's feet and spray them with vodka, and then the women stomp the grapes. The following year, the participants return and buy the wine they helped make.

Although White Crane's wines have won many awards, the owners say "the biggest thrill is seeing the smiles on our customers' faces when they try our wines." They are proud, also, of the many charity events hosted at the winery. "It is a great feeling to help when you can."

In addition to the high-end White Crane label, Nardolillo offers a more affordable array of wines under his Winery 21 label (named in honor of being the twenty-first winery to open in the Livermore Valley), whose price point ranges from $12 to $19.

Their winemaking style is predicated on the maxim that great wine starts in the vineyard. "From there, through various techniques, we try and bring out the true flavors that Mother Nature gave me that particular year," they says. "Our job is to retain the wine's healthy essence."

Half of White Crane's wines are estate grown, and the the winemakers are downright surgical in their quest for maximum flavor components in his grapes. To achieve this, they will drop an incredible amount of fruit. A field that might produce seven to eight tons per acre will net just over two tons after cluster thinning. They also cold soak their grapes for a week to maximize the flavor transfer from skins to juice. This also serves to soften the tannins, creating an early sense of a well-aged product.

White Crane wines exhibit caramel, vanilla, and spice flavors that are intensified by his use of 30 to 35 percent new oak barrels, while the rest are neutral oak barrels (a combination of French, Hungarian, and American oak).

A visit to White Crane Winery, perched 900 feet up on a hillside, is well worth the journey. You can savor award-winning wines while looking out over panoramic vistas of vines undulating down the hillsides to the spread of Livermore Valley fields below.

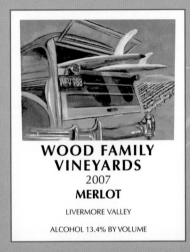

WOOD FAMILY VINEYARDS
2007
MERLOT
LIVERMORE VALLEY
ALCOHOL 13.4% BY VOLUME

Wood Family Vineyards
7702 Cedar Mountain Drive
Livermore, CA 94550
(925) 606-7411

Website:
woodfamilyvineyards.com
Email: rhonda@
woodfamilyvineyards.com
Facebook and Twitter

- Tasting room: by appointment and for scheduled events
- Established: 2000
- Owners: Rhonda (winemaker) and Michael Wood
- Annual production: 1,500 cases
- Varieties: Petite Sirah, Cabernet Franc, Cabernet Sauvignon, Merlot (estate grown), Zinfandel, Syrah, Chardonnay, Grenache
- Wine club: Extended Family Member

It's all Good at Wood

*R*aised in Fremont, California, Rhonda Wood was a licensed private pilot by the age of seventeen. Continuing her aviation studies, she was accepted at Embry-Riddle Aeronautical University in Prescott, Arizona, where she also served as a flight instructor at the local airport. After graduation, she went to work as a commercial pilot for US Airways. On a successful early path of his own, her husband, Michael, graduated from Berkeley with a degree in finance and then took off to tour Europe and work at Squaw Valley for a few years before settling down in the corporate world.

The Woods' introduction to the world of wine actually began with beer and germinated while Rhonda was grounded during her first pregnancy. "I decided to make home-brew beer—I had heard an old wives' tale that beer was good for breast milk," she remembers.

Back in the cockpit after bearing her second child, Rhonda thought, "What are we doing making beer? We drink more wine than beer. I should be making wine."

Wood Family Vineyards

So back at home in Fremont, they planted Cabernet and Zinfandel grape vines in their backyard overlooking Weibel Vineyards, with the intention of making wine—all the while fostering images of purchasing a winery upon retirement. Before the vines reached maturity, Rhonda participated in the Livermore Valley Wine Country Harvest Festival—and that's where the real epiphany struck.

Photo courtesy of The Independent Magazine

Parker, Harrison (back row), Michael and Rhonda Wood, and T-Bone

"I suddenly realized that this great wine country was right in our backyard! And then I saw a Merlot vineyard for sale. It suddenly dawned on me—we don't have to wait for retirement. We can afford to buy this land now! We can keep our day jobs and jump right in!" And that's exactly what they did.

With one barrel, Rhonda started making Merlot home wine in 1996. "The funny part," she says, "is that we did not even drink Merlot at the time. We went out and did extensive research and discovered that we really liked it a lot."

The Woods' vines produce small berries, and thus their Merlot has lots of intensity, great tannin structure, and excellent fruit concentration. The end product is a bold, really big style Merlot.

In 2000, their winery was bonded, and they started out producing 160 cases a year. Rhonda was still flying for US Airways, but in the aftermath of September 11, 2001, she was given a five-year leave of absence. She eventually retired from the airline to focus full time on her family and their vineyard. Today, they produce 1,800 cases annually.

On top of Michael's daily commute to work in Sunnyvale, he maintains all of the winery equipment and handles the books. "He is my strong back during crush, and he is often a one-man press machine," Rhonda says.

In addition to Wood Family Vineyards' estate Merlot, all of their grapes are sourced from nearby growers, and Rhonda keeps an eagle eye on her berries as they mature. Don't be surprised if you see her zooming around the valley and through the vine rows onboard her mountain bike to check out the progress of her contracted grapes.

Of the ten varieties produced by the Wood family, Rhonda enjoys every one but raves about her Chardonnay. "It has crisp acidity and full malolactic fermentation, so it has more complexity and it's aged in 100 percent French oak."

When she first crafted the Chardonnay, she remembers with a joyful chuckle, "I named it Para Mas Amigas, assuming it meant For My Girlfriends. But it turns out it actually means For More Girlfriends—so of course I have more girlfriends now, and everyone loves it!"

Rhonda is also a fan of Zinfandel because of the many different styles. "We make a spicy, old vine Zin that has the pepper goin' on—black peppers, white peppers. And there's my Hanson Ranch Zinfandel that's a great fruit bomb, but not too jammy."

Pleasant surprises are part of the adventure for Rhonda. She first started using Grenache to blend with Syrah, but they liked it so much they now produce it on its own. The same thing happened with their Cabernet Franc. It was originally selected for a Bordeaux blend, but now it's also its own star.

The Woods enjoy their many friends and family members who come out for all of the events and help at harvest and crush. "That makes it all so worthwhile," Rhonda says. "The Woody on our label personifies quality, family, friends, and fun—and we believe life should be approached with this in mind."

Growers

Amante Vineyards *
Arroyo/Aero Properties, LLC
Barnett Vineyards *
Bear River Ranch *
Buttner Sunol Valley Vineyard
LLC *
Casa de Vinas *
Circle H Vineyards *
Clark Vineyard
Coastal Viticultural Consultants *
Del Arroyo Vineyards, LLC
Falling Star Vineyard *
Fraser Vineyards
Frydendal Brothers Vineyards *
Galles Vineyard *
Ghielmetti Vineyard *
Gustavino Vineyard
HLW, LLC *

Irwin Vineyards *
Las Positas Ranch(TKG) *
PICAZO Vineyards *
Pinnacle *
Rigg Estate Vineyard *
Roboli Ranch
Scarlet Bear
Shannon Vineyards
Sblendorio Vineyards*
Sun Hill Vineyard *
Tarantino Vineyards *
Tazetta Vineyard *
Thatcher Bay Wineyards *
Triska Crane Ridge Vineyards *
Tri-Valley Vineyards LLC *
Vista Diablo Vineyards *
Walker Ranch Vineyard *
Wisner Vineyards *

*Livermore Valley Winegrowers Association Member

Photo by John Montgomery

A Taste of
Things
to Do & See
in Livermore Valley

First Street Wines
2211 First Street
Livermore, CA 94550
(925) 294-5825

FIRST STREET WINES

Website: www.wineco.com
Email: steward@wineco.com

Jeff Jewett's First Street Wines is centrally located in the heart of downtown Livermore and carries a selection of excellent wines from Livermore Valley, as well as those from top producers and small boutique wineries from around the world. Stop in and check out their broad selection of value-priced premium wines.

Towne Center Books
555 Main Street
Pleasanton, CA 94566
(925) 846-8826

Website: www.townecenterbooks.com
Email: info@townecenterbooks.com

Judy Wheeler has created a community center at her charming Towne Center Books, and the locally owned store is a happening

place on Pleasanton's Main Street. Everyone is welcome to have tea, discuss books, join one of the book clubs, or attend the Read It and Eat luncheon series, where authors talk about their texts. In December, youngsters gather for the Breakfast with Santa in the large and roomy children's section. And for those wanting to pen their own prose, there are writing groups.

Swirl on the Square
21 South Livermore Avenue
Livermore, CA 94550
(925) 447-1400

Website: www.swirlonthesq.com
Email: Rocco@swirlonthesq.com

Swirl on the Square, a hip wine lounge located in historic Blacksmith Square, showcases local wines paired with sumptuous tapas, dinnertime entrees, and desserts. Owner Rocco Maitino offers a memorable Livermore wine country experience in a relaxed setting, where guests are served tapas and wines from outstanding local vintners, including Steven Kent, Retzlaff, el Sol, Thomas Coyne, Cuda Ridge, Wood Family, Occasio, Longevity, and Crooked Vine. For an outstanding accompaniment, be sure to order his Swirl Classic—triple cream brie with prosciutto di Parma, fig jam, and arugula on a sourdough baguette. Equally tempting is the slow-cooked pulled pork with guacamole, chipotle mayo, queso fresco casero, and cilantro served on a fresh bun.

Primarily showcasing the distinctive wines of Livermore Valley, Swirl is a recommended destination for couples and small groups

looking for a place to kick back and savor exceptional vino paired with outstanding culinary treats. The historic setting features local art and family photos that grace the century-old, patina-tinged brick walls. Be sure to ask for Rocco's mother's Secret Cake. There's a cult following for this specialty dessert.

The Wine Steward
641 Main Street
Pleasanton, CA 94566
(925) 600-9463
Website: www.thewinesteward.com
Email: Jim@thewinesteward.com

The Wine Steward, housed in the old Roxy Theater in downtown Pleasanton, is the largest wine shop in the East Bay—displaying some 1,000 selected wines from around the world. Upstairs at the fragrance-free wine bar, visitors sip wines and even partake in wine appreciation classes. "We try to show customers the world of wine. We meet everyone where they are and urge them to take a step further, hopefully expanding their horizons," says General Manager Jim Denham. "We love to show people our wines."

Niles Canyon Railway's Wine Tasting on the Rails
(925) 862-9063
Website: www.ncry.org

Niles Station
37001 Mission Blvd.
Fremont, CA 94536

Sunol Depot
6 Kilkare Road
Sunol, CA 94586

Today, trains on the Niles Canyon Railway roll down the same tracks as those that first steamed through Niles Canyon on the original trailblazer Trans-Continental Railway back in 1869. You can ride those rails and sip Livermore Valley wines thanks to the Niles Canyon Railway's Wine and Cheese special.

While riding through the most pristine countryside in the San Francisco Bay Area, wine educator Steve Ferree pours local wines and pairs them with hors d'oeuvres as he narrates stories of the region and Livermore Valley vintners.

The train stops twice, once atop the historic Farwell Bridge so that passengers can drink in the bucolic landscape and the leafy Alameda Creek. Sometimes they catch sight of wild turkeys, deer, coyotes, and maybe a fox or a golden eagle.

Nearly one hundred years ago, passengers might have seen the likes of Charlie Chaplin. From 1912 to 1916 Niles Canyon was home to Essanay Film Studios, where Chaplin made his celebrated movie *The Tramp*.

The Wine and Cheese Special is carefully choreographed each year by Bob Bradley. He and Ferree take their own tasting group to Livermore Valley wineries to scout out twenty-four or so excellent varieties. A typical selection for the ride includes two whites and three reds (different wines are featured every week) with carefully selected cheeses, breads, and chocolates to complement each. Passengers receive a commemorative wine glass and special buffet tray to keep.

In addition to the Wine and Cheese Special, Niles Canyon Railway—staffed entirely by volunteers—offers regular, roundtrip runs between Fremont and Sunol on Sundays throughout the year. These trips are open to the public, and some passengers stop over in either town for a meal or shopping and return on a later train.

A highlight of the holidays, the Train of Lights begins the day after Thanksgiving and runs through December. Thousands of lights adorn the inside and outside of the train, dazzling some 20,000 passengers each year. A favorite treat is the hot chocolate sold at the snack bar—and of course the bearded, jolly fellow in red who gives out candy canes during the ride is always a big hit.

Vino Cellars & Accessories
2241 First Street
Livermore, CA 94550
(925) 447-8000
fax: (925) 447-8015

Website: www.vino-cellars.com
Email: info@vino-cellars.com

Vino Cellars & Accessories specializes in custom wine cellar design and installation, temperature-controlled wine cabinets, wine coolers, and accessories—everything but the wine! If you have a closet or pantry that you want to convert into a cellar, Vino Cellars will assist you with CAD drawings free of charge. Simply fax or email the dimensions, and they'll send your drawing within three to five days.

Vino Cellars also offers a wide array of self-contained, furniture-style, temperature-controlled wine cabinets—including credenza upright styles with capacities ranging from 58 to 2,500 bottles.

Vino Cellars is located in downtown Livermore. Showroom hours are 10 a.m. to 5 p.m., Tuesday through Friday; 11 a.m. to 5 p.m., Saturday; and by appointment on Sunday and Monday evenings. You can also shop online at their website listed above.

Events

Harvest Wine Celebration
(925) 447-WINE (9463) (weekdays only)

www.lvwine.org

Held on Labor Day weekend

Harvest is always an exciting time in Livermore Valley wine country. This annual tradition features more than forty wineries, each hosting music, crafts, wine tasting, food, activities, and more. Visitors party along the Livermore Valley Wine Trail by car or free shuttle. The award-winning celebration is the largest wine event in Livermore Valley and serves as the annual fundraiser for the Livermore Valley Winegrowers Association.

Photo by Steven Kelly

Taste of Terroir: Livermore Valley's Wine & Food Experience
(925) 447-WINE (9463) (week-days only)

www.lvwine.org;

Held the third Thursday in July

Join Livermore Valley winemakers and Bay Area chefs as they team up to create innovative pairings featuring local wines and foods from the valley's terroir. Guests cast their votes for the People's Choice Award, and culinary and media judges present awards in other categories. In addition to the pairings, the event features a wide array of desserts, a silent auction, and more. Get tickets early, as this event sells out.

Holidays in the Vineyards
(925) 447-WINE (9463) (weekdays only)

www.lvwine.org

Held the first weekend in December

Celebrate the season with a weekend full of holiday cheer. Wineries showcase their festive, decorated tasting rooms with arts and crafts vendors, holiday music, special wines, food pairings, visits from Santa, and more. Tasting fees vary by winery.

San Ramon Art & Wind Festival

www.ci.san-ramon.ca.us

Held Memorial Day weekend

The San Ramon Art & Wind Festival happens every year on the Sunday and Monday of Memorial Day weekend, from 10 a.m. to 5 p.m. The festival includes 200 arts and crafts booths, professional kite-flying demos, kite-making workshops, more than twenty food and beverage booths, a huge kids' area, and entertainment on three stages. A hot air balloon launch is featured on Sunday morning at 6 a.m.

The Livermore Valley Wine Auction
(925) 447-WINE (9463)
(weekdays only)

www.lvwine.org / Held the first weekend in May

The Livermore Valley Winegrowers Foundation raises funds for local children's charities through its annual wine auction. Guests enjoy a gala evening of bold culinary dishes and award-winning wines from the valley. Silent and live auctions showcase Livermore Valley wines along with travel, sports, art, and adventure packages. Over the past fifteen years, the Winegrowers Foundation has raised more than $3.4 million to support local children's charities.

The annual event is produced in conjunction with the Livermore Valley Winegrowers Association and the generous support of countless volunteers.

Livermore Rodeo
(925) 455-1550 /
(925) 447-3008

www.livermorerodeo.org
secretary@livermorerodeo.org

Held the second weekend in June

Cowboys and fans ride into town every year for the Livermore Rodeo. This steer-riding, calf-roping contest has been called the Fastest Rodeo in the World. "We have fifteen chutes," says Christie Dixson, secretary/director of the Livermore Stockmen's Association. Out of these chutes come the bravest, craziest cowboys around. The event takes place at Robertson Park.

Photo by Steven Kelly

Barrel Tasting Weekend
(925) 447-WINE (9463)

www.LVwine.org
Takes place in March

Wine enthusiasts enjoy wines right out of the barrel, meet winemakers, purchase futures, and other activities during Barrel Tasting Weekend. In addition to barrel samples, guests can indulge in various weekend activities at participating wineries including: bottle your own wines, food and wine pairings, cooking demonstrations, barrel taste comparisons using different oaks, winemaker discussions, and more.

With the hills lusciously green and vines just starting to bud, this is an excellent time of year to visit Livermore Valley Wine Country. There are a limited number of tickets available each year.

Additional Events

Alameda County Fair, Pleasanton, *www.alamedacountyfair.com*

Downtown Wine Festival, Livermore, *www.livermoredowntown.com*

Fine Arts Faire, Danville, *www.danvilleareachamber.com*

Fourth of July Parade, Danville, *www.kiwanis-srv.org/parade.asp*

Fourth of July Star-Spangled Spectacular, San Ramon,
    www.ci.san-ramon.ca.us/parks/

Goodguys National Car Shows, Pleasanton, *www.good-guys.com/events*

Halloween Carnival, Livermore, *www.livermoredowntown.com*

International Children's Film Festival, Danville, *www.caiff.org/danville*

Spring & Fall Wine Strolls, Danville, *www.discoverdanvilleca.com*

St. Patrick's Day Festival, Dublin, *www.dublinstpats.com*

Summer Farmer's Markets: *Danville, Livermore, Pleasanton, San Ramon*

Summer Wine Stroll, Pleasanton, *www.pleasantondowntown.net*

Truffles & Tidbits, Pleasanton, *www.pleasantondowntown.net*

Photo by Thomas C. Wilmer

Theater

Livermore Valley Performing Arts Center
Bankhead Theater
2400 First Street
Livermore, CA 94550
(925) 373-6800

www.livermoreperformingarts.org

Performances at the state-of-the-art Bankhead Theater include opera, ballet, concerts, plays, speakers' series, and more. The 500-seat theater houses many of the area's finest performing arts organizations, including Del Valle Fine Arts, Livermore Valley Opera, California Independent Film Festival, Livermore-Amador Symphony, Valley Dance Theater, Cantabella Children's Chorus, Tri-Valley Repertory Theatre, and the Valley Concert Chorale. The theater also hosts visiting performance ensembles from around the Bay Area and provides performance and recital space for local music, dance, and theatrical training programs.

Photo by Thomas C. Wilmer

Livermore Shakespeare Festival
(800) 838-3006
www.livermoreshakes.org

Held in the summer

Under the stars at Concannon Vineyards, enjoy a magical performance at the Livermore Shakespeare Festival. Ticket prices and performances vary. Tickets go on sale in the spring.

Village Theatre
233 Front Street
Danville, CA 94526
(925) 314-3400

Website: www.villagetheatreshows.com

Dougherty Valley Performing Arts Center
10550 Albion Road
San Ramon, CA 94582
(925) 973-2787

Website: ci.san-ramon.ca.us/parks/theater/venues.htm

Livermore Valley Wine and Cycle Tours
1462 Groth Circle
Pleasanton, CA 94566
(925) 399-6751

Website: www.livermorewineandcycletours.com
Email: barbara@livermorewineandcycletours.com
Saturday and Sunday, 11:30–3:30

Cycle through the beautiful Livermore Valley wine country and stop along the way to sip local wines, taste local olive oils, and enjoy a gourmet lunch. Bring your own bike or rent one from Cyclepath in Pleasanton (http://cyclepath.com; [925] 485-3218). Tour guides will pick up and return rentals.

Photo by Barbara Mallon

Hiking in Livermore Valley

Nestled in a circle of mountains, Livermore boasts the largest regional/municipal park system in the country. The wide range of native flora, trees, and wildlife is bountiful, and opportunities for hiking are endless on the area's well-established ranch roads and single-track paths. The spectacular terrain and outstanding views make it a destination spot for those in the entire bay region, not just locals.

The trails weave through a mosaic of extensive oak woodlands, annual grasslands, and seasonal wetlands. These natural habitats are home to myriad endemic wildlife species, including fox, elk, bobcat, deer, and coyote. If it's your lucky day, bald eagles may embolden themselves and come out of hiding at Del Valle. You'll get your fill of the area's beautiful flora, as well: abundant wildflowers bloom in this region from February into the summer.

The trailheads described in this section may all be reached within five to thirty minutes by car and are located on both the north and south sides of Livermore. Bicycles are permitted on many of the trails listed here, and, with the exception of Los Vaqueros, so are dogs.

For a more extensive look at hiking in Livermore Valley, I recommend the book *Tri-Valley Trails*, by Nancy Rodrigue and Jacky Poulsen. This handy guidebook offers descriptions of more than seventy-five trails in ten Tri-Valley parks and is available for purchase at Livermore Valley bookstores and wineries.

Trails

The trails listed here offer exceptional views of Livermore Valley. At each trailhead you will find maps with additional paths for the more adventurous hiker. You can also visit www.ebparks.org and www.larpd.dst.ca.us for more information.

Del Valle Regional Park

Heron Bay/Dam Trail

Level of difficulty: moderate

Getting there: Drive south to the end of Arroyo Road and turn left into the parking lot. There is a parking fee.

Details: The hike is only 1.5 miles but there is a steep climb of 500 feet. You can easily extend your visit here by dropping down to Lake Del Valle from several of the Heron Bay marked trails.

The trail: From the parking area, walk through the cattle gate. The trail is straight ahead and dips down to a bridge that crosses a stream. From there it is mostly uphill. At the top, there is a spectacular view of the South Livermore Valley, the Wente Golf Course, and Lake Del Valle. You'll return on the same trail.

Photo by Barbara Mallon

Rocky Ridge Trail
Level of difficulty: strenuous

Getting there: Drive south on Mines Road and bear right onto Del Valle Road. Continue about three miles to the kiosk. There is a parking fee. From the kiosk, drive ahead and cross the bridge. Turn left and pass the campground entrance. You'll then turn right onto a gravel road and right again into the unpaved parking area.

Details: This is a four- to five-mile hike with a total elevation gain of 1,900 feet.

The trail: Find the narrow Vallecito Trail across from the entrance of the parking lot. This winds its way along a beautiful shady riparian creek up to a sign-in panel. From there, you'll begin an uphill climb on an old ranch road. Eventually, it will split. The right leg of the trail leads to Stromer Spring. Continue climbing to the top of the ridge. The trail bends to the left and follows the ridge. There are spectacular views of the lake, the valley, and the interior mountains. Wildflowers bloom beginning in February and lasting well into late spring.

Continue along the ridge and follow the trail as it turns to the left. This begins the long descent with views all the way. Be sure to turn right at the bottom of the first hill, skipping Stromer Spring. You'll find yourself back at the sign-in panel, where you can sign out and turn right onto Vallecito Trail, which leads back to the parking area.

Sycamore Grove Park

Valley View Trail

Level of difficulty: moderate

The Valley View Trail offers beautiful vistas of the south Livermore vineyards and beyond. The remains of an old winery and home site provide a glimpse into Livermore's rich wine history.

Getting there: Drive south on Arroyo Road and turn right onto Wetmore Road. The park entrance is located on the left at the bottom of the hill. There is a parking fee.

Details: This is a 3.5-mile hike with a total elevation gain of 650 feet.

The trail: From the parking lot, step onto the paved trail and cross the bridge. Just beyond, bear right onto an unpaved road called Winery Loop Trail. This follows the southern edge of the park, passes by a ranger's house, and leads to an intersection with Walnut and Wagon Road Trails. Continue a few more feet and bear right up the hill lined with old olive trees onto Wagon Road Trail. This eventually turns sharply to the right.

Turn left onto Valley View Trail, which presents a steep uphill climb to the viewpoint. On the return, backtrack down to Wagon Road Trail and turn left. Stay on this trail as it connects back to Winery Loop Trail. Turn left and retrace your steps or take Walnut Trail straight ahead to the paved trail. From there, you can turn left to return to the parking area.

Photo by Barbara Mallon

Brushy Peak

Brushy Peak Loop Trail

Level of difficulty: easy to moderate

Hop on this trail to enjoy exceptional valley views from the north looking south. This site is also home to a working ranch and a restored wetland.

Getting there: Drive north on Greenville Road, go under the freeway, and turn left. Turn right at the first street you come to, Laughlin Road. This is a very narrow, one- to two-lane road. Follow it to the end, and turn right into the parking lot.

Details: This is a 6.3-mile hike with a total elevation gain of 1,200 feet.

The trail: Walk back down the driveway and cross the road, and you'll see where the trail begins. Shortly after the trailhead, bear right onto Westside Loop Trail and follow the wetland preserve

Photo by Barbara Mallon

north toward Brushy Peak. When the trail begins to climb, take the first branch to the right: it's a footpath and the beginning of Brushy Peak Loop Trail. This path climbs over a small hill just below Brushy Peak then descends. Turn left onto Tamcan Trail and then left onto Laughlin Ranch Trail for a little more climbing, or continue straight on the Brushy Peak Loop Trail. Both lead back to the trailhead.

Los Vaqueros Lake

Valley View Trail

Level of difficulty: moderate

This hike begins with views of distant lakes and ends with a pleasant ridgeline walk with views of rolling hills and ranchlands to the north.

Getting there: Drive north on Vasco Road, cross the freeway, and continue driving north for three miles. After passing the dump on the right, watch for the very small sign on the left announcing Los Vaqueros Lake. Turn left and drive to the kiosk. There is a parking fee. Park in the first area on the left.

Details: This is a 6-mile hike with a total elevation gain of 1,160 feet.

Photo by Barbara Mallon

Photo by John Montgomery

Lawrence Livermore National
Laboratory Discovery Center
Building 651 Eastgate Drive
(off Greenville Road)
Livermore, CA 94550
(925) 423-3272
www.publicaffairs.llnl.gov/com/discovery_center.html

As a visitor, you can see an overview of the lab's world-class scientific programs. Ride the energy bike and generate your own electricity, explore earthquake computers, check out the Richter scale, and handle the world's lightest manmade substance—Aerogel.

Sunol Water Temple
505 Paloma Way
Sunol, CA 94586
www.sunol.org/temple.html

Modeled after the Temple of Vesta in Tivoli, Italy, the sixty-foot edifice has twelve Corinthian columns, a red tile roof, and a ceiling that's painted with the motif of Indian maidens carrying water vessels.

The beaux art pavilion was designed by San Francisco architect Willis Polk in 1910 for the Spring Valley Water Company. At that time, half of San Francisco's water supply passed through the temple. In 1989, its roof was severely damaged in the Loma Prieta earthquake and was removed, and the temple closed to the public. The columns began to deteriorate, and there was talk of tearing the temple down. A group of Sunol citizens stepped in and publicized the temple's crumbling state. Eventually the Public Utilities Commission responded and restored it. Today, the San Francisco Water District owns the temple, but very little fresh water flows through it. However, it remains a lovely California monument that's open to the public on weekdays from 9 a.m. to 3 p.m.

The Carnegie Museum and Art Gallery
2155 Third Street
Livermore, CA 94551
(925) 449-9927
www.livermorehistory.com/Carnegie Museum/Carnegie Museum.html

This is one of the many beautiful, classical libraries the Andrew Carnegie Foundation funded around the United States in the early 1900s. Its doors first opened in 1911. Today, the historic library houses the Livermore History Center and a beautiful gallery featuring local artists' work, including oils, watercolors, textiles, jewelry, pottery, and more.

Photo by Thomas C. Wilmer

Eugene O'Neill's Tao House
PO Box 280
Danville, CA 94526
(925) 838-0249

www.eoneill.com/eof/tao_house/visit.htm

Admission is free to this historic site, where Nobel Prize-winning playwright Eugene O'Neill lived and worked. Tao House is set in a beautiful, pristine environment, which O'Neill chose so that he could concentrate on writing. Reservations by phone are required. If there is no answer, leave a voice-mail message. Directions will be provided when your reservation is confirmed. The National Park Service provides a shuttle for the short ride to the site.

Photo Courtesy of The Eugene O'Neill Foundation

Photo by Thomas C. Wilmer

Ravenswood Historical Site
2647 Arroyo Road
Livermore, CA 94550
(925) 373-5708
(weekdays only)
www.larpd.dst.ca.us/
rentals/ravenswood.html

On the National Register of Historic places, this restored Victorian estate was built in the 1880s and was once one of the valley's largest vineyards. It's open to the public on the second and fourth Sunday of each month from noon to 4 p.m., and docents offer free tours on these days. (It's closed, however, the fourth Sunday in December.) Ravenswood is available to rent for private parties.

Blackhawk Museum
3700 Blackhawk Plaza Circle
Danville, CA 94506
(925) 736-2280
www.blackhawkmuseum.org

This 70,000-square-foot museum opened in September 1988 to showcase some ninety classic cars from all over the world. Today, its two 2,100-square-foot galleries offer rotating exhibitions. The museum also offers educational lectures, an automotive research library, and a bookstore.

Centennial Light Bulb
Fire Station #6
4550 East Avenue
Livermore, CA 94550
(925) 454-236

www.centennialbulb.org

Livermore's Centennial Light Bulb is the longest burning bulb in history. With more than one hundred years of illumination, it was declared the oldest known working light bulb by the *Guinness Book of World Records*. Visitors can view the bulb, which has been illuminated since 1901, if the firemen at Station #6 are available at the time. Go to the rear of the station and ring the bell. If no one answers, look through the window and up to the left—and there you will see the glowing bulb.

Photo by John Montgomery

Golf

The Course at Wente Vineyards
5040 Arroyo Road
Livermore, CA 94550
(925) 456-2477

Website: www.wentevineyards.com

Pay a visit to The Course at Wente Vineyards, and you'll enjoy a world-class, par-seventy-two course that wanders over hills, across small valleys, and through vineyards. Phil Wente partnered with Aussie champion Greg Norman to create this scenic but challenging course, which opened in 1998.

The opening tee shot drops one hundred feet into a sunken valley. Before teeing off at the first hole, golfers gaze out at the Cresta Blanca cliffs on one side of the hill and the sweeping vistas of Livermore Valley on the other. As part of its nationwide tour, the PGA has held the Livermore Valley Wine Country Championship at Wente Vineyards, and PGA competitors ranked the course as the toughest on the tour, but they also named it one of their favorites.

After a game, golfers often stop for classic American grilled food—and wine, of course—at The Grill next to the 18th green. The Wente family says The Grill is modeled after an Australian station house, reminiscent of Greg Norman's childhood in the outback.

The Wente's sealed their pairing of golf and wine when Swedish-born LPGA champion Annika Sörenstam teamed up with fifth-generation winemaker Karl Wente to create the new premium syrah, Annika, which debuted in 2009.

Poppy Ridge Golf Course
4280 Greenville Road
Livermore, CA 94550
(925) 447-6779
Website: www.poppyridgegolf.com

The beautiful Poppy Ridge Golf Course in South Livermore comprises twenty-seven holes divided into three nines. In recognition of the wine country that surrounds it, Poppy Ridge has named its courses Zinfandel, Chardonnay, and Merlot.

A sister to Monterey's celebrated Poppy Hills course (which cuts through wooded country), the Poppy Ridge layout is in the Scottish heathland style: wide open with rolling hills, a few trees, and ponds. Some of the higher spots make for stunning valley vistas.

"It's a fun course," says General Manager Todd Cook. The heathland design is challenging, he says, because of the rolling hills. "You get a lot of roll on your ball."

"The rough is rough," adds Player Assistant Steve Erdman. "The bunkers are difficult, as well—typical of a heathland course." The three-course rotation increases player capacity by 50 percent. "You can play eighteen holes here in four hours and fifteen minutes," he says.

Poppy Ridge also offers a full-service restaurant, Porter's, which serves up Kobe beef burgers, salads, sandwiches, pastas, and a captivating view of the course. The beautiful setting and Porter's elegant restaurant in the mission-style clubhouse make Poppy Ridge Golf Course a popular place for weddings and events.

Callippe Preserve Golf Course
1306 Happy Valley Road
Pleasanton, CA 94566
(925) 426-6666
www.playcallippe.com

Golfweek magazine listed Callippe as one of the Best Municipal Golf Courses in the Nation for 2008–2009. Open since November 2005, Callippe is part of a cooperative effort to create an unusual amalgamation—an eighteen-hole golf course, hiking and equestrian trails, endangered species habitat, wetland establishment, and dedicated grazing land. The Vista Restaurant in the clubhouse offers breakfast and lunch daily, along with a sweeping view of the course.

Sunol Valley Golf Club
6900 Mission Road
Sunol, CA 94586
(925) 862-2404
www.sunolvalley.com

The Sunol Valley Golf Club is one of the most affordable in the Bay Area. Set along the hills adjacent to the 680 freeway, the club features two courses, a clubhouse, a driving range, and food and beverage services. Sunol Valley Golf Club also offers facilities for weddings and special events.

Las Positas Golf Course
917 Clubhouse Drive
Livermore, CA 94551
(925) 455-7820
www.laspositasgolfcourse.com

This affordable municipal course is walkable and challenging, with seven lakes and a creek that splits multiple holes. Along with its par-seventy-two, eighteen-hole course, Las Positas has a nine-hole executive course with two lakes, a driving range, putting green, and food and beverage services.

San Ramon Golf Club
9430 Fircrest Lane
San Ramon, CA 94583
(925) 828-6258
www.sanramongolfclub.net

This eighteen-hole course in the San Ramon hills offers beautiful views and a wide array of wildlife. The ninth hole is on an island green. The course is easily walked, though power carts can be rented. Either way, the course can be completed in 4.5 hours or less. The San Ramon Golf Club also offers a clubhouse, driving range, swimming pool, and food and beverage services.

Canyon Lakes Golf Club
640 Bollinger Canyon Way
San Ramon, CA 94582
(925) 735-6511
www.canyonlakesgolfclub.com

The golf course at Canyon Lakes Country Club in San Ramon is an eighteen-hole championship course that also offers incredible vistas of Mt. Diablo and the San Ramon Valley.

The course is open to the public on weekdays. Starting times may be arranged up to seven days in advance. Tournament play may be arranged by calling Monday through Friday, between 7:30 a.m. and 5:00 p.m., or Saturday and Sunday, between 7:00 a.m. and 5:00 p.m.

Photo by John Montgomery

Restaurant at Wente Vineyards
5050 Arroyo Road
Livermore, CA
(925) 456-2450

Website: www.WenteVineyards.com

When the Wente family added the historic Cresta Blanca winery property to their assemblage of vineyards in 1981, they breathed life back into its long-neglected sandstone caves and vines. The Wentes wanted to create something special there on Arroyo Road, and this wide nook in the hills is one of Livermore Valley's most beautiful spots.

The Restaurant at Wente Vineyards, the vision of fourth-generation family member Carolyn Wente, opened in 1986 and has become an icon of Livermore Valley's fine dining scene. Modeled on
her family's tradition of wine and food as an integral part of daily
life, she designed her menu to offer the freshest local ingredients
available—years before it became the trend. "We are so fortunate
to have such an abundance of fresh produce available right here in
Livermore Valley," she says.

The art in Wente's craft of fine food preparation is predicated on
"combining and using the ingredients respectfully to bring out the
best flavors, without overdoing it," she says" Balanced foods go
beautifully with balanced wines. "This makes for an exquisite meal
and brings the dining experience to the next level." Ultimately, it's
a matter of attention to detail—from the food and wines to the
service. "That's what makes for a seamless dining experience for
our guests, and that's what we're all about," Wente says."

Chefs harvest produce from the winery's garden or buy it from
the local farmers market, and menu offerings change according to
the seasons and what's ripened.

The restaurant is replete with rich woods, large windows, and
French doors overlooking an expansive patio with umbrella tables.
Oak, palm, and sycamore trees are nestled in close, with the vine-
yards just beyond.

The sprawling lawn alongside the restaurant is a popular site for
weddings and summertime concerts, where headliners include Tony
Bennett, Ringo Starr, Chris Isaak, James Taylor, Sheryl Crow, and
comedians Dana Carvey and Kathy Griffin. Sometimes, as they did
during the B-52s concert, the winery rolls out the dance floor. On
select summer eves, the same lawn fills up with blankets and picnic
baskets as families sprawl on the grass for big screen movie night.

The Wentes have added yet another piece to their repertoire.
Fifth-generation family member Karl, a vintner, chemical engineer,
and musician, is pairing wine with music. While learning to play

the guitar, Karl found that the sensual experiences and creation of wine and music are similar. His project, "Discover the Wine, Discover the Music," pairs wine varietals with the tempo, immediacy, and mood of music. About one pairing, he says, "The flavors linger in a beautiful way—the same way that the song, especially the guitar, lingers in your mind. . . ."

Chef Kimball Jones and Carolyn Wente received so many requests for their recipes they decided to collaborate on a cookbook, *Sharing the Vineyard Table: A Celebration of Wine and Food from the Wente Vineyards Restaurant*. The incredible response to their endeavor led to a second book, *The Casual Vineyard Table*. "It's a collection of food that goes great with wine that I put on the table every day, in less than an hour, she says."

Wente Vineyards has evolved over the years to become a destination all its own. Amenities include a world-class, Greg Norman-designed golf course, a stunning tasting room, a Spanish-Colonial-style event center, a concert series, movies in the park, and ample wedding venues. And, of course, the award-winning Restaurant at Wente Vineyards promises you an unforgettable dining experience in the heart of Livermore Valley wine country.

Café Garré at Garré Vineyard and Winery
7986 Tesla Road
Livermore, CA 94550
(925) 371-8200
www.garrewinery.com

Drive through the lantern lit iron gates of Garre' Winery and you will experience the Molinaros family hospitality on a property rich with history. The charming Cafe Garre' is a dream come true for executive chef, Ty Turner, who has been at Garre' since the cafes opening.

A sunny dining room with arched doorways, racked wines and murals set the stage for a Brushy Peak Sandwich, Pasta Pomodoro, or one of many other yummy items on the menu. "Mediterranean-meets west" is how Turner, who teaches Art Culinare at the Art Institute in Sunnyvale, describes his menu. "We are fortunate here in the Bay Area for the fresh produce and sea food available. I love to create oyster and smoked fish or meat dishes." Estate-grown organic herbs and specialty heirloom vegetables are also emphasized.

Set among the vineyards is the patio, where diners can escape the hustle and bustle and enjoy the peaceful surroundings. Across the lawn is the clapboard house which was a speakeasy during prohibition. The property was a prestigious horse ranch in it's hay day where crooner Bing Crosby stayed while his wife Dixie Lee received treatment in the old Livermore Sanitarium. Now the house serves as the office and the porch is home to local musicians during the summer Dine and Music on the Patio series every Friday night.

Turner, who also writes a regular column on wine pairings for D'Vine Magazine says,"When you are pairing wines and salads you have to be careful to balance the acidic component." He marinates black figs in Garre's Cabernet Franc for his popular Wine Country Mixed Salad, and said the salad pairs well with a red wine.

Looking north, beyond the café is a century old oak tree, surrounded by lawn and flowers, it has been the perfect spot for many weddings with the reception to follow in the tented pavilion. Seated at the top of the hill behind the winery is the beautiful hacienda-style Martinelli Center. The Molinaro's are contracted by the county of Alameda to cater meetings and weddings there as well.

Café Garré is open for lunch Monday through Friday from 11:00 am–2:30 pm; Saturday and Sunday from 11:30 am–3:30 pm. During the summer, they offer Dine and Music on the Patio on Friday nights and Italian Dinner and Bocce every Wednesday and of course several special Winemaker dinners throughout the year.

Campo di Bocce
175 E. Vineyard Avenue
Livermore, CA 94550
(925) 249-9800

Website: www.campodibocce.com
Twitter: http://twitter.com/Livermore_Bocce
Facebook: Campo di Bocce

Imagine a venue that combines world-class bocce courts with a traditional Italian restaurant and full-service bar. Only a handful of such establishments exist in the United States, and Campo di Bocce of Livermore is one of them. The sprawling, Tuscan-style restaurant offers traditional Italian fare served up by an award-winning chef—and eight state-of-the-art bocce courts.

Campo di Bocce sits in the Ruby Hill vineyard at the gateway to Livermore wineries. Chief Operations Officer Ben Musolf says, "We are a premier dining experience and a showcase for bocce."

He also explains that the game is called bocce, not bocce ball. "It's like you say golf, not golf ball."

Musolf should know; he's coached two world-championship teams and hosted international tournaments at Campo di Bocce. He says it's the second fastest growing sport (after soccer) for amateurs in the U.S. Bocce is played in basements, backyards—anywhere. But Campo di Bocce flew in an expert from Italy to build its courts, four of which lie inside the restaurant and four on the patio amid dining tables and a vine-covered arbor.

In addition to his bocce expertise, Musolf is a level II sommelier and teaches the art of wine tasting. "You have two hands," he says, "one for the bocce ball and one for wine." Cheers drift in from the patio as a bocce ball rolls right up to the *pallino*.

Musolf says some customers come just for the food, wine, and ambiance. Some come just for bocce and some for all of it.

Hall of fame coach John Madden and former coach of the San Francisco 49ers Steve Mariucci sponsor the Madden-Mariucci Charity Bocce Tournament here each year.

Campo di Bocce is the brainchild of Tom Albanese, who opened the successful Campo di Bocce of Los Gatos in 1997. Musolf,

COO of both venues and son-in-law of Albanese, has overseen the building and development of the Livermore facility, which opened in 2006.

Embracing the surrounding wine country, Campo di Bocce hosts winemaker dinner and bocce tournaments. They also offer a Picnic in the Vineyards take-out menu of cheeses, breads, and meats. And those who stop in for a meal can bring their own bottle. There's no corkage fee for local wines.

While visiting the world-class wineries and vineyards of Livermore Valley, be sure to stop in at Campo di Bocce for a little world-class, Italian-inspired diversion.

Barone's Restaurant
475 St. John Street
Pleasanton, CA 94566
(925) 426-0987
www.themenupage.com/baronesrestaurant.html
Dinner (lunch offered weekdays)

Barone's Restaurant offers romantic, elegant ambiance with candles, a fireplace, patio, live music in the bar, and, in the summer, a courtyard with music and fire pits. The longtime staff is welcoming, and the service is good. Barone's continental menu with an Italian flair is excellent. The restaurant provides room service for the Rose Hotel.

Photo by Thomas C. Wilmer

Photo by Thomas C. Wilmer

Hap's Original Steaks & Seafood
122 W. Neal Street
Pleasanton, CA 94566
(925) 600-9200

Website:
www.hapsoriginal.com
Email:
manager@hapsoriginal.com

Dinner only

This longtime Pleasanton eatery offers certified Angus steaks aged twenty-one to twenty-eight days, seafood dishes, specialty desserts, and an award-winning wine list. You can also enjoy a drink in the bar or by the fireplace, and you may just see owners Michael Connors, Paris Connors, and James Wilson—as well as chef Wilson Miller—mingling with the customers.

The Farmer at the Pleasanton Hotel
855 Main Street
Pleasanton CA, 94566
(925) 399-6690

Website:
www.pleasantonhotel.com
Email:
info@pleasantonhotel.com

Lunch, dinner, and Sunday brunch

Photo by Thomas C. Wilmer

Housed in the historic and charming Pleasanton Hotel (built in 1864), The Farmer offers up American fare, including steak, fish, and chicken. The Farmer's busy events calendar offers Karaoke nights and live music. You can also enjoy one of the bar's many drink specials while watching a game on the TV.

Blue Agave Club
625 Main Street
Pleasanton, CA 94566
(925) 417-1224

Website:
www.blueagaveclub.com

Lunch and dinner (summers); dinner Tuesday through Saturday (winters)

This longtime Pleasanton restaurant resides in a 140-year-old Victorian house with a broad front patio. Blue Agave serves up "high" Mexican fare, with offerings ranging from tortilla soup and mole poblano to grilled salmon and filet mignon. They also specialize in sipping tequilas and offer a list of more than 200.

Photo by Thomas C. Wilmer

Photos by Thomas C. Wilmer

Oasis Grille and Wine Lounge
780 Main Street
Pleasanton, CA 94566
(925) 417-8438
www.oasisgrille.com
Lunch and dinner

This exotic eatery in downtown Pleasanton offers Mediterranean cuisine, including kabobs, lamb, and Moroccan stuffed chicken, as well as vegetarian dishes. You can also enjoy exotic cocktails such as a Cubano Mojito or Pom Island Iced Tea in the lounge or the beautiful rose garden.

Pasta's Trattoria
405 Main Street
Pleasanton, CA 94566
(925) 417-2222
www.pastastrattoria.com
Lunch and dinner

Whether sitting in the window or at one of the sidewalk tables, Pasta's customers enjoy the people watching on Pleasanton's Main Street. They also enjoy the authentic Italian cuisine, of course, which includes hand-tossed pizzas and excellent pastas. The creamy and rich Caesar salad makes an excellent first course, and Pasta's tiramisu is a great way to finish the meal.

Dean's Café
620 Main Street
Pleasanton, CA 94566
(925) 846-4222
Website: www.deanscafe.net/
index.html
Email: deanscafe@yahoo.com
Breakfast and lunch only

Photo by Thomas C. Wilmer

After fifty years in business, this greasy spoon is still a favorite of locals and a good place for breakfast. Aside from the usual breakfast and lunch menu items, the list of omelets at Dean's is nothing short of spectacular. The one hundred or so choices include Polish, Portuguese, Mexican, hot-pepper, mortadella mushroom, and more. The cooks here will grill, fry, and boil just about anything a customer wants.

Faz
600 Hartz Avenue
Danville, CA 94526
(925) 838-1320
Website: www.fazrestaurants.com
Email: Danville@fazcatering.com
Lunch and dinner

This popular and elegant Danville restaurant is set in a redwood grove, with floor-to-ceiling glass in the lounge and dining room. While there, be sure to enjoy a pizza or flatbread from the wood-burning oven and one of the scrumptious housemade desserts. Faz, which offers up Italian-Mediterranean fare, also has locations in Pleasanton, Palo Alto, and Sunnyvale.

Esin Restaurant & Bar
In the Rose Garden Center
750 Camino Ramon
Danville, CA 94526
(925) 314-0974
www.esinrestaurant.com
Lunch and dinner

Co-executive chefs Curtis and Esin de Carion's restaurant consistently gets top reviews. The menu offers American fare with a Mediterranean influence and includes pot roast braised in veal stock; grilled, dry-rubbed rib eye; and filo-wrapped chicken breast filled with three cheeses. Esin creates the desserts—baklava, black bottom white chocolate banana cream tart, cheese dishes, and more. *Wine Spectator* and *Wine Enthusiast* magazines have recognized their extensive California wine list. The staff is friendly and the ambiance relaxing and elegant.

Bridges Restaurant and Bar
44 Church Street
Danville, CA 94526
(925) 820-7200
www.bridgesdanville.com
Lunch and dinner

On most everyone's top-ten list, Bridges offers up California-American cuisine with influences from Europe and Asia. The menu features local, organic ingredients when available. Dine inside in an urban-casual setting or on the patio in the summer while listening to live music.

Amber Bistro
500 Hartz Avenue
Danville, CA 94526
(925) 552-5238

www.amberbistro.com

Lunch
Dinner on Saturday
and Sunday

Amber Bistro owner Eric Janssen, a certified sommelier, boasts perfect pairings of excellent wines with California cuisine. The affordable menu offers fresh, seasonal ingredients, and the ambience is sophisticated yet casual. Amber Bistro has a full bar and offers complementary valet parking in the evening.

McNamara's Steak and Chop House
7400 San Ramon Road
Dublin, CA 94568
(925) 833-0995

www.mcnamarasrestaurant.com

Dinner only

This Chicago-style chophouse serves American fare, including mid western corn-fed Angus beef, aged for a minimum of twenty-one days. Fish is delivered fresh daily. Located near the junction of Highway 580 and 680, McNamara's is within a few miles of most hotels.

Izzy's Steaks & Chops
200 Montgomery Street
San Ramon, CA 94583
(925) 830-8620

www.izzyssteaks.com

Dinner only

A sister to the famous Izzy's in San Francisco, the San Ramon restaurant opened in 2007 and offers Izzy's classic American cuisine, including steaks, chops, and seafood. Locally owned and operated, Izzy's also offers a location in San Carlos.

Terra Mia Cucina Italiana
4040 East Avenue
Livermore, CA 94550
(925) 456-3333

Website: www.terramiarestaurant.com
Email: info@terramiarestaurant.com

Situated in a strip mall, this restaurant is a pleasant surprise with its lovely Tuscan ambiance. It's a dream come true for owners Roberto and Giovanni, who were born and raised in the south of Italy. Their menu offers traditional fresh pastas, sauces, meats, cheeses, and wines.

Lodging

THE ROSE
HOTEL

The Rose Hotel
807 Main Street
Pleasanton, CA 94566
(925) 846-8802/(800)
843-9540

Website: www.rosehotel.net
Email: info@rosehotel.net

Over the past twenty-five years I have been on numerous assignments around the globe as an international travel journalist, and I have stayed at some of the world's finest five-star hotels, from Marrakech and Monte Carlo to London, Hong Kong, and Bora Bora. So I can say with confidence that the Rose Hotel in the sleepy little town of Pleasanton is truly world-class.

The understated elegance, attention to detail, and value-added amenities are peerless. There's a long list of five-star in-room touches, including Aveda bath products, Swiss truffles on the down pillows, French press Peet's coffee, 410-thread-count linens, scented candles, two-person whirlpool spas, and separate walk-in showers. Complimentary amenities throughout the Rose include a fitness room and guest passes to a nearby full-service athletic club, free wireless Internet access, laptops and printers for in-room use, concierge services, and more.

Exit the velour-lined elevator en route to your room, and you're greeted by a credenza with fresh fruits and snacks. A spiral-bound notebook awaits you on the in-room work desk. Another in the long list of giving gestures at the Rose, it's yours to keep.

Even the lobby experience is loaded with indulgent, pleasant gratis surprises, including bottled water, fresh Peet's coffee, and tea at the ready—around the clock. You'll also find a jar of fresh cookies, mini candy bars, and Red Vines licorice. In the morning, you'll savor the ample continental breakfast included in your stay. In the afternoon and evening, there's a lobby wine bar for your enjoyment.

The human element at the Rose is equally memorable, from the sincerely friendly front desk personnel to the housekeeping staff. Praise is due to General Manager Phylis Grisham for her detail-oriented management style and especially to the John Madden family, who are the owners and visionaries behind every nuance of the Rose experience.

Coach Madden's son, Mike, says, "Dad is very well-traveled, and when we created the vision for the Rose we got together with our architect and delineated the design elements for our new hotel—with all the touches of a place that our family would love staying

Photo by Thomas C. Wilmer

in and appreciate." For example, they specified oversized Jacuzzi tubs, "where you can actually stretch out," as well as separate, spacious, marble-lined walk-in showers.

Central to the Madden family's approach was the melding of a welcoming environment with the sophistication of a fine hotel and the warmth and comfort of an elegant home. Throughout the hotel you'll see endless evidence of the family's deft touches—including understated interior design elements, handsome woodwork, sophisticated fur-

nishings, lush fabrics, and original artwork on the walls.

Another attraction is the Rose Hotel's central location. It's right in the heart of downtown Pleasanton—one of the quaintest and most charming, people friendly small towns you'll encounter in California. You can easily leave your car in the covered parking garage for the duration of your stay and have an exciting weekend getaway without traveling further than two or three blocks. Numerous restaurants with al fresco dining line Main Street, and two top picks, The Farmer and Barone's are adjacent to the Rose. .

If you come to stay, be sure to inquire about the hotel's wine getaway experiences, which include a Meet the Winemaker package, as well as customized wine getaways crafted to the guests' sensibilities and desires.

Four Points by Sheraton
5115 Hopyard Road
Pleasanton, CA 94588
(925) 460-8800

www.fourpoints.com/pleasanton

With lagoons, waterfalls, fountains, and nearby shopping, this beautiful hotel is located in the Hacienda Business Park near the 580 and 680 freeways, central to Livermore Valley. Among other amenities, the hotel offers free high-speed Internet, comfortable beds, and free bottled water. The property is 100 percent smoke-free.

Marriott Pleasanton
11950 Dublin Canyon Road
Pleasanton, CA 94588
(925) 847-6000

www.marriottpleasanton.com

The recently remodeled Marriott Pleasanton caters to the demands of business guests and wine-country vacationers alike. For those on holiday, the hotel offers an Escape to Wine Country Package with a complimentary bottle of local wine in your room.

Purple Orchid Inn Resort & Spa
4549 Cross Road
Livermore, CA 94550
(925) 606-8855
www.purpleorchid.com

The setting for this rustic, elegant inn and spa (the only bed & breakfast in the entire Livermore Valley) is a twenty-one-acre olive orchard nestled in the valley's wine country. Fountains, a swimming pool, hot tubs, flagstone walkways, Tuscan décor, and the plentiful roses and greenery create a beautiful getaway. Thanks to this enchanting setting, the ten-room Purple Orchid has hosted more than a thousand weddings. A health and wellness destination, the Purple Orchid offers spa packages, including bio-organic treatments. The Poppy Ridge Golf Course and many Livermore wineries are nearby.

Hawthorn Suites Livermore Wine Country Hotel
1700 N. Livermore Avenue
Livermore, CA 94551
(925) 606-6060
www.hotellivermore.com

The Hawthorn Suites Livermore Wine Country Hotel is centrally located, offering guests all that the valley has to offer. Your stay at the hotel will include a full, hot buffet breakfast each morning and an evening social hour Monday through Thursday that features local wines. The hotel has sixty-two spacious studio suites and offers complimentary high-speed wireless Internet, an outdoor pool and indoor whirlpool, and a full fitness center.

The hotel's vacation packages are the perfect way to escape, combining a night's stay with featured wine tastings, rounds of golf, tickets to performances at the Bankhead Theater, dinners at local restaurants, and discounts on downtown Livermore shopping and dining. The Wine Country Getaway Package is a popular choice for wine seekers and includes:

- One night's stay in a king or double-queen studio suite
- Wine pairing for two at La Rochelle Winery
- One bottle of fine Livermore Valley wine
- Complimentary appetizer at Zephyr Grill & Bar
- Downtown guest pass with discounts at participating businesses
- Full, hot buffet breakfast
- Access to the indoor whirlpool, outdoor heated pool, and fitness center
- Complimentary evening social hour Monday through Thursday

Visit www.hotellivermore.com for complete package listings and details.

Courtyard by Marriott
2929 Constitution Drive
Livermore, CA 94551
(925) 243-1000
www.marriott.com/oaklm

Doubletree Hotel Livermore
720 Las Flores Road
Livermore, CA 94550
(925) 443-4950
www.livermore.doubletree.com

Hilton Garden Inn Livermore
2801 Constitution Drive
Livermore, CA 94550
(925) 292-2000
www.hiltongardeninn.com

Holiday Inn (formerly Radisson)
6680 Regional Street
Dublin, CA 94568
(925) 828-7750

Photo by Thomas C. Wilmer

The Wine Seeker's Guide to Livermore Valley

Visitor's Resources

Bureaus and Associations

Livermore Valley Winegrowers Association
3585 Greenville Road, Suite 4
Livermore, CA 94550
(925) 447-9463
www.LVwine.org

In 1981, threatened by impending development, a small group of vintners and growers formed the Livermore Valley Winegrowers Association. Today with a membership of more than sixty wineries and growers, the association is dedicated to showcasing the Livermore Valley wine country by highlighting the talent, energy, fine wine, and visitor amenities of this American Viticultural Area (AVA).

Just forty-five minutes east of San Francisco, Livermore Valley wine country welcomes visitors with a flourish expanse of vineyards, wineries, and wine country experiences.

The lush vines and convivial tasting rooms increasingly define the quality of life in the valley and, to the delight of residents and visitors alike, the region is enjoying a wine renaissance harking back to the golden years of early California wine history.

Spanish missionaries planted the first wine grapes in Livermore Valley in the 1760s. In the 1840s, California pioneers looking for outstanding vineyard sites also began planting grapes in the region. Robert Livermore planted the first commercial vines in the 1840s, and later pioneer winemakers C.H. Wente and James Concannon recognized the area's winegrowing potential and founded their wineries in the early 1880s.

Attracted to the rich winemaking tradition, geography, soil and climate, new winemakers and vineyardists are working alongside fifth-generation winegrowers to create this Livermore Valley wine renaissance.

The region now has more than forty wineries and counting, and more than 5,000 acres of vineyards. Wineries vary in size from limited-release, 100-case labors of love to 400,000-case industry heavyweights. Grapes range from familiar Merlot and Chardonnay to Italian, Rhone, and Spanish varieties. Welcoming tasting rooms showcase award-winning wines and offer year-round activities. In addition to the myriad happenings at individual wineries, the Livermore Valley Winegrowers Association sponsors several consumer events each year, showcasing the talent, energy, and fine wines of the region.

Tri-Valley Convention and Visitors Bureau
349 Main Street, Suite 203
Pleasanton, CA 94566
(925) 846-8910

www.trivalleycvb.com (For information about Pleasanton, Livermore, Dublin, San Ramon, and Danville)

Danville Chamber of Commerce
117 Town and Country Drive
Danville, CA 94526
(925) 837-4400

www.danvilleareachamber.com

Livermore Chamber of Commerce
2157 First Street
Livermore, CA 94550
(925) 447-1606

www.livermorechamber.org

Pleasanton Chamber of Commerce
777 Peters Avenue
Pleasanton, CA 94566
(925) 846-5858

www.pleasanton.org

San Ramon Chamber of Commerce
12667 Alcosta Boulevard
San Ramon, CA 94583
(925) 242-0600

Website: www.sanramon.org
Email: info@sanramon.org

Photo by John Montgomery

Livermore Valley Wine Country–an established American Viticultural Area (AVA)

Livermore Valley is a recognized official growing region that has been certified and registered by the Federal Alcohol, Tobacco, Tax, and Trade Bureau (TTB) as America's seventeenth American Viticultural Area (AVA).

The Livermore Valley AVA geography encompasses the valley floor and the encircling hills of Alameda County, as well as the southern part of Contra Costa County. Cities within the AVA include Danville, Pleasanton, Livermore, San Ramon, and the eastern boundaries of Castro Valley and Sunol.

Each AVA encompasses unique climatic conditions, soil compositions, etc. Official AVA designation allows consumers to make educated purchasing decisions on the origin of grapes in their wine. Presently there are more than 187 AVAs in the United States, including Napa Valley, Paso Robles, Monterey, Lodi, and, of course, Livermore Valley. For a complete list of AVAs, visit www.iwineinstitute.com.

—Livermore Valley Wine Growers Association

eed a break from wine tasting? There's no shortage of diversion in Livermore Valley. You can go for a hike or bike ride, shop, browse art galleries, catch a play or concert, enjoy fine cuisine, and more. Explore the towns of Livermore Valley and beyond to enhance your wine country experience.

Castro Valley

www.castrovalleychamber.com

Castro Valley, an unincorporated bedroom community, is approximately thirty miles equidistant between San Francisco and San Jose. Bordered by San Leandro, Union City, and Dublin, Castro Valley is easily accessed by Interstate 580, 880 and BART (Bay Area Rapid Transit system).

The areas first inhabitants were the Ohlone Indians. Following Spanish colonial rule, the area came under the purview of Mission San Jose. The town was named after Don Guillermo Castro, a former Mexican Army soldier who was granted the sprawling 28,000-acre Rancho San Lorenzo by the Mexican government. Castro Valley's modern history evolved when chicken ranching was introduced in the early 1900s. By the 1960s agrarian enterprises were supplanted by real estate development and housing tracts. Today Castro Valley is primarily a bedroom community of 58,000 residents, with many commuting to work in the Silicon Valley and throughout the San Francisco Bay Area. Among the local attractions is the Adobe Art Center, a public gallery dedicated to showcasing fine artists from the region. Outdoor enthusiasts savor Cull Canyon Park, a popular spot that offers swimming, fishing, and picnicking. If you're into biking, be sure to check out the nearby Lake Chabot Loop mountain bike trails.

Danville

www.ci.danville.ca.us

Known as the "Heart of the San Ramon Valley," Danville offers the perfect blend of upscale amenities and small-town charm. Its quaint character and convenient location just thirty miles east of San Francisco make it the perfect place to work, live, and play. With a population of approximately 43,250, Danville is known for its small-town atmosphere and outstanding quality of life.

The historic downtown features shops, restaurants, and art galleries that draw people from all over. You'll find epicurean adventures around every corner—including upscale eateries with one-of-a-kind menus and pizzerias with family-friendly fare. Arts and culture experiences await you at the Village Theatre, the Museum of the San Ramon Valley, and Tao House—dedicated to America's only Nobel Prize-winning playwright, Eugene O'Neill.

One of Danville's most desirable attributes is its sense of community. The town hosts a wonderful array of events throughout the year, from farmers markets to street fairs to holiday celebrations. The town's highly rated schools, executive homes, and unending recreational activities (which include hiking, biking, swimming, and more) add to Danville's unparalleled appeal.

Photo by Candace Rana

Dublin

www.ci.dublin.ca.us

From the Ohlone Indian tribe who once roamed this rich valley to the Irish immigrants who gave it its name, Dublin is a place with a wealth of history. Dublin values its roots yet embraces its future and the potential that comes with growth. Gracing fourteen square miles at the crossroads of I-580 and 680, Dublin is a blend of rolling hills and scenic flatlands with extraordinary vistas of Mt. Diablo and Donlon Point. During your visit, you can explore the vast hiking and biking trails or take advantage of the many parks—fourteen in all—that offer something for everyone. Home to the largest skate parks in the Tri-Valley area at Emerald Glen Park, Dublin is currently creating a historic park to complement the city's Heritage Center activities.

In addition to Dublin's splendid recreational and sporting facilities, the city has entertainment and shopping to rival any in the area. Dublin and its surrounding communities offer excellent retail

outlets—from malls with national and regional chain stores to neighborhood plazas with specialty shops. The Hacienda Crossings Shopping Center also offers a twenty-one–screen movie complex. It's the largest in the Tri-Valley area—complete with a state-of-the-art IMAX screen.

Livermore

www.ci.livermore.ca.us

Founded in 1869, Livermore is framed by award-winning wineries, farmlands, and ranches that mirror the valley's western heritage. The city of Livermore (population 83,604) encompasses twenty-two square miles. As the easternmost city in the San Francisco Bay Area, it's known as the gateway to the Central Valley. Protection by the coastal range provides Livermore with a mild climate that enhances the pursuit of a relaxed, uncongested lifestyle.

Home to two renowned science and technology centers—the Lawrence Livermore National Laboratory and Sandia National Laboratory—the city is a technological hub and an academically

Photo by Thomas C. Wilmer

engaged community. Powered by its wealth of research, technology, and innovation, Livermore has become an integral part of the Bay Area and a success at competing in the global market.

Livermore's arts and culture, western heritage, and vibrant wine industry create a unique community. The historic downtown area is enjoying a renaissance, reestablishing itself as the city's preeminent shopping, dining, entertainment, and cultural district with a new ten-screen cinema and 500-seat performing arts center. With the addition of several residential projects, art/live workspaces, and a pedestrian-friendly environment, Livermore offers an active urban experience for visitors and residents of the valley.

Pleasanton
www.ci.pleasanton.ca.us

Downtown Pleasanton is the perfect setting for festivals, street parties, parades, weekly summer concerts, Saturday farmers markets, and other special events. Notable for its small-town ambience

Photo by Thomas C. Wilmer

accented with a sophisticated metropolitan edge, Pleasanton offers some of the finest dining and shopping in the area. And it's also home to the Alameda County Fairgrounds, which hosts the annual county fair, as well as statewide and regional events.

Residents and visitors enjoy convenient access to jobs, shopping, entertainment, recreation venues, and more. Outdoor opportunities abound: more than 1,200 acres are dedicated to forty-two beautifully groomed neighborhood and sports parks, and twenty-two miles of trails offer spectacular vistas of the Bay Area from hillside peaks, the Iron Horse Regional Trail, and the award-winning Callippe Preserve Golf Course. Get a taste of the city's rich history by visiting the Museum on Main Street or the restored Alviso Adobe interpretive park.

Main Street in downtown Pleasanton is widely recognized as one of the most charming historic retail destinations in the region, featuring a mix of unique shops and restaurants. And the nearby Stoneridge Mall features more than 165 specialty stores and restaurants, including P.F. Chang's and The Cheesecake Factory.

A free summer concert series, outdoor movies, a weekly downtown farmers market, and, coming soon, a center for the performing and fine arts are among the many amenities that contribute to Pleasanton's distinctive appeal. Located at the junction of I-580 and 680, Pleasanton is just an hour away from many famous Bay Area destinations, including San Francisco, Monterey, and Berkeley's nationally recognized Gourmet Ghetto.

San Ramon

www.sanramon.ca.gov

San Ramon is a dynamic, vibrant city nestled in the rolling hills of the Tri-Valley region. Central Park is the heart of the city and home to the Art & Wind Festival held every May. It's also where you can throw a blanket on the grass and enjoy Fourth of July fireworks and other outdoor concerts and events. The farmers market at historic Forest Home Farms, which offers fresh produce, flowers, and crafts, runs May through November. Forest Home Farms also offers annual activities for the whole family to enjoy, including tours and special events.

Visitors can tee off at the city's multiple golf courses, which include the Canyon Lakes and San Ramon Golf Clubs. If you're up for a challenge, visit Bridges Golf Club, rated one of the most difficult courses in Northern California. But whether you're looking to test your skills or take a more leisurely stroll on the green, all three courses offer great golfing and venues for your special wine country event.

While you're visiting, be sure to catch one of the many San Ramon Performing Arts shows offered at the Dougherty Valley Performing Arts Theater, which is currently celebrating its third season. From dance and musical performances to Broadway plays, San Ramon Performing Arts has something spectacular for everyone. An annual series features popular artists such as Boyz II Men and David Benoit. For upcoming event and show information, visit www.sanramonperformingarts.com or call (925) 973-ARTS.

Before or after a show, you can also experience fabulous dining at a reasonable price. Download listings and reviews of San Ramon restaurants at www.sanramon.ca.gov/econdev/restaurant.html.

Sunol

www.sunol.net

Sunol, a sleepy village of 1,300 denizens, dates from the mid-1800s. Farmers and ranchers were the mainstay of this place until the advent of the Transcontinental Railroad in 1869. With a station stop in Sunol, the village gained popularity as a vacation destination for city dwellers in the San Francisco Bay Area. In 1871 the town was redubbed Sunolglen but reverted to Sunol in 1920. By 1900 the town boasted four hotels, two restaurants, two barbershops, and a soda fountain.

Although several fires over the past century have destroyed more than eight structures in town, there remains a timeless, twilight-zone quality to this bucolic burg. The circa-1925 Sunol School is a visual slice of the past, as is the charming UCC Little Brown Church on Kilkare Road.

Sunol made international news when Bosco, a Labrador Retriever, was elected mayor in 1981. He served until his death in 1994.

A leisurely visit to the little town of Sunol is a must-do, and be sure to stop by the vintage Southern Pacific Depot, circa 1884. If time allows, hop aboard the Niles Canyon Railway for a wine train adventure featuring Livermore Valley selections. Sunol is just one mile from I-680 near the Livermore and Pleasanton exits.

Photo by Thomas C. Wilmer

Soils of the Livermore Valley

The soils in the Livermore area are formed from a variety of sedimentary and igneous rock types. In the vicinity of Mount Diablo and in the southeastern part of the county are relatively small areas of metamorphic rock. The Contra Costa Hills to the west and the Mount Diablo range to the north and east are composed chiefly of Tertiary and Cretaceous strata. These rocks consist of sandstones, limestones, conglomerates, and argillaceous shales. Nearly all of the soils in the area have formed in the weathering products of these rocks and have been subsequently modified by the processes of erosion, movement, and deposition.

Based principally on topography, the soils fall naturally into two groups, upland soils and valley soils.

The upland soils are primarily residual soils derived from the underlying bedrock. The most extensive residual soils are mapped as Altamont clay, Diablo clay, Linne clay loam, Los Osos loam, and Vallecitos loam. Altamont clay (Vertisols) and Diablo clay (Vertisols) are derived from the decomposition of the underlying calcareous sandstones and shales, principally of the Tertiary age. Linne clay loam (Mollisols) is derived chiefly from the decomposition of underlying limestones and calcareous sandstones and shales. Los Osos loam (Mollisols) is derived from the decomposition of sandstone. Vallecitos loam (Alfisols) is derived from the decomposition of metamorphic rocks.

The valley soils are alluvial, alluvial wetland, and largely colluvial mixed with alluvial material. The most recently formed, alluvial soils are classified as Yolo loam (Entisols) and Livermore gravelly loam (Mollisols). The alluvial wetland soils are Fluvaquents. The mixed alluvial and colluvial soil type on older stream terraces is mainly Pleasanton gravelly loam. Most of the area's vineyards are planted in these valley soils.

——Thomas J. Rice, PhD, C.P.S.S.
   Professor of Soil Science
   Certified Professional Soil Scientist No. 1932
   California Polytechnic State University

Sources
1. H. L. Westover and Cornelius Van Duyne, *Soil Survey of the Livermore Area*, California, (USDA Bureau of Soils, 1910).
2. L. E. Welch et al., *Soil Survey of Alameda Area*, California, (U.S. Government Printing Office, 1966).

About the Author

Author, travel writer and photographer Thomas C. Wilmer started his journalism career as a copy boy for the West Coast edition of *The Wall Street Journal* while attending college in the San Francisco Bay area. He's logged over a million miles in his travels across the globe, from Morocco to China, up to the Arctic Circle and down to South Africa. Wilmer's words and photography on world-wide and West Coast destinations have appeared in numerous lifestyle magazines. His newspaper travel features have appeared across North America on the Knight Ridder Wire Service, including Toronto, Phoenix, Salt Lake City, Savannah, St. Paul, Annapolis, and Tampa. Wilmer's radio travel show, *Audiolog—The Travel Show* (awarded "Best Radio Show" by Outdoor Writers Association of California in 2007) has aired over California Central Coast National Public Radio (NPR) affiliates for more than twenty years. In 2007 he was awarded the Henry Lawson Travel Writing Award Grand Prize by Tourism Australia/Qantas for the best North American media travel destination feature about Australia. The recipient of Santa Cruz County Conference and Visitors council's PRIDE award, he was also awarded "Best Magazine Feature" 2nd place in 2007 by Outdoor Writers Association of California. Wilmer is a member of the (San Francisco) Bay Area Travel Writers' Board of Directors, a member of International Food, Wine and Travel Writers Association, and Outdoor Writers Association of California.